Insomnia Solutions

A New Approach to Achieving Restful Sleep Through Cognitive Behavioral Therapy (CBT), Diet and Nutrition, and Prayers for Peace

Danielle Pataky

© **Copyright 2022 - All rights reserved.**

The content contained within this book may not be reproduced, duplicated or transmitted without direct written permission from the author or the publisher.

Under no circumstances will any blame or legal responsibility be held against the publisher, or author, for any damages, reparation, or monetary loss due to the information contained within this book, either directly or indirectly.

Legal Notice:

This book is copyright protected. It is only for personal use. You cannot amend, distribute, sell, use, quote or paraphrase any part, or the content within this book, without the consent of the author or publisher.

Disclaimer Notice:

Please note the information contained within this document is for educational and entertainment purposes only. All effort has been executed to present accurate, up to date, reliable, complete information. No warranties of any kind are declared or implied. Readers acknowledge that the author is not engaged in the rendering of legal, financial, medical or professional advice. The content within this book has been derived from various sources. Please consult a licensed professional before attempting any techniques outlined in this book.

By reading this document, the reader agrees that under no circumstances is the author responsible for any losses, direct or indirect, that are incurred as a result of the use of the information contained within this document, including, but not limited to, errors, omissions, or inaccuracies.

Table of Contents

INTRODUCTION 1

CHAPTER 1: SLEEP ON IT 3

    THE SCIENCE OF SLEEP 3
    IMPORTANCE OF SLEEP 5
    STAGES OF SLEEP 6
    SLEEP CHANGES ACROSS YOUR LIFESPAN 8
    SLEEP QUALITY VS. SLEEP QUANTITY 9
    SLEEP DEPRIVATION AND DEFICIENCY 10

CHAPTER 2: FEELS LIKE INSOMNIA 13

    OVERVIEW OF INSOMNIA 13
    CAUSES OF INSOMNIA: THE 3P MODEL 14
    OTHER CAUSES OF INSOMNIA 15
    TYPES OF INSOMNIA 18
    TREATMENT OPTIONS 19
        Medication 20
        Cognitive Behavioral Therapy 21
    MY STORY 22

CHAPTER 3: CHECK YOURSELF 25

    KEEP A SLEEP DIARY 25
    DETERMINE DISRUPTORS 27

CHAPTER 4: COGNITIVE BEHAVIORAL THERAPY FOR INSOMNIA 33

    COGNITIVE BEHAVIORAL THERAPY FOR INSOMNIA 34
    MY STORY 37

CHAPTER 5: RESTRICT AND CONTROL 39

    SLEEP RESTRICTION 39
        Guidelines and Implementation 40
        Sleep Restriction Tips 41
    STIMULUS CONTROL 42
        Rationale and Implementation 43

CHAPTER 6: QUESTION YOUR MIND 45

    COGNITIVE DISTORTIONS & IMPACT ON SLEEP 45

    Cognitive Restructuring 46
    Implementation 47
    Challenge Common Negative Sleep Beliefs 48
    Schedule Worry Time 49
    My Story 50

CHAPTER 7: CLEAN SWEEP FOR CLEAN SLEEP 52
    Sleep Hygiene Recommendations 53
    Product Suggestions 54
    Low-Income Sleep Hygiene 56

CHAPTER 8: KICK BACK AND RELAX 59
    Relaxation Techniques 59
    Journaling for Sleep 63
    On the Go 65
    Relaxing Morning Routines 67
    Relaxing Bedtime Routines 70
    Try This Out! 73

CHAPTER 9: GOOD FOOD, GOOD NIGHT 75
    Diet and Nutrition 75
    The Link Between Sleep and Nutrition 77
    Foods to Avoid Before Bed 78
    Foods that Help You Sleep 78
    More Nutrition Tips 79
    Sleep-Friendly Exercise 82
    My Story 83

CHAPTER 10: LET GO AND LET GOD 85
    Prayer and Sleep 85
    Prayers for Comfort and Peace 86
        For When You are Anxious 86
        For When You are Afraid 87
        For When You Forgive or Ask for Forgiveness 87
        For When You Need Sleep and Rest 88
    Additional Prayers 89
    My Story 91
    Secular Aid 91

CONCLUSION 95

REFERENCES 97

Introduction

"Innocent sleep. Sleep that soothes away all our worries. Sleep that puts each day to rest. Sleep that relieves the weary laborer and heals hurt minds. Sleep, the main course in life's feast, and the most nourishing." – William Shakespeare, Macbeth

A third of your life is meant to be spent sleeping. The time you spend asleep is one of the most important parts of the day; sleep is where you heal, process, and rest. A soft, pillowy bed and a warm blanket can feel like a much deserved hug after a long day, and the rest that comes after can seem like nirvana. Those eight hours you lay down to rest are immensely valuable, but many of us know the struggle associated with chronic insomnia. For a lot of us, sleep is evasive–something we long for but are unable to quite reach.

When you miss out on valuable sleep, your physical and mental health suffer, but it is very likely that you already know this if you suffer from insomnia for any length of time. You may be familiar with feeling irritated and sluggish, and want nothing more than to sink back into bed, yet when you do so you are unable to fall asleep. Nothing you try works, and it is incredibly frustrating. One of the most natural and necessary bodily functions seems to be running from you as hard and fast as it can. You might be ready to try anything just for a few moments of true, blissful rest. I know exactly how this feels.

Today is the day that all of these feelings come to a halt. From here on out, you are sure to get closer and closer to a good night's sleep, because this book holds every solution to your struggles with insomnia. You will learn the right approaches to mind, body, and spiritual healing that you have been missing out on to cure your insomnia. This is a holistic approach that others adore and have described as the only true relief to their chronic insomnia struggles. It has taken me decades to gain and improve upon these methods, one's that hundreds of former insomniacs now speak highly of. People who have followed this miracle holistic approach have said they do not obsess about sleep all day long anymore, and that they feel like a whole new person when they wake up.

You too can feel this way. Imagine a life where you wake up refreshed and energized and go about your day feeling amazing. Your stress has melted away, and your ambition and passion have returned to everything you do. All of your interactions are enthusiastic and you are bursting with a love for life. The whole day goes smoothly, and you come home feeling accomplished. You kick up your feet to relax, and then head to bed a little while later. That feeling of dread and exasperation that clung so tight to you is now behind you. You look forward to each new accomplishment with a smile and pride. Your body sinks into the soft expanse of your bed, you shut your eyes comfortably, and sleep well for a solid eight hours before waking up and doing it all again.

This is how I feel every day after developing my personal approach to insomnia, and I am going to share that approach with you too. Insomnia plagued me for so many years, but now I go to bed and wake up a whole new person every single day. My mind, body, and soul are so much better for it. Reaching this stage seemed impossibly hard before I mastered it, and my hope is to make that process simple for you. A lot of trial and error, doctor's visits, appointments, medication, and other struggles have gone into figuring out what does and does not work against the woes of insomnia. Throughout the course of this book, I will give you all of the secrets you need to turn your life around and get the sleep you deserve. It is time to take back your sleep and live the rest of your life feeling refreshed and elated, every single day.

Chapter 1:
Sleep on It

Human beings are the only mammals that purposefully avoid going to sleep at night in favor of engaging in other activities. Before the development of technology such as the lightbulb, the internet, social media, and streaming services that many of us enjoy daily, it was normal and even expected for humans to sleep at least nine hours a night. That might sound insane if you are someone who is used to the harsh treatment of chronic insomnia, but the sleep patterns of people about one hundred years ago are scientifically more natural for us human beings. These sleep patterns went unhindered by distraction because people slept when they needed to, a luxury many of us can incorrectly assume we do not have.

Understanding the role science plays in our sleep is one of the most important ways to begin to understand your insomnia itself. Science is a third of the battle in completely relieving insomnia. The body is a complex being and far more factors play into what causes sleep or lack thereof to occur. Familiarizing yourself with some of the basics of sleep science is vital. Strong knowledge regarding why and how people slept so soundly before society was inundated with ceaseless distraction is going to be incredibly useful in starting your journey towards a life with restful sleep.

The Science of Sleep

Most people are not actually sure what sleep really is. It is obvious that sleep is a period of rest, but what is the body actually doing while we are asleep? How does sleep work? Science can answer that question thoroughly, and understanding that answer is important to bettering your journey towards an insomnia free life. Sleep impacts the various systems of your body, including your immune and digestive system.

Failure to get enough sleep at night can cause anything from general tiredness to such severe outcomes as heart and breathing issues. This explains why you feel groggy, irritable, or even sick when you miss out on a good night's rest; failing to get enough sleep night after night is one of the worst things you can do to your body.

There are two main processes that the body uses to regulate your sleep: sleep drive and the circadian rhythm cycle. Sleep drive can also be referred to as homeostatic sleep drive and is the term that is used to describe the mental process responsible for increasing your desire to sleep the longer that you have been up (Meistad, 2022). For someone with a healthy sleep drive, it is expected that they will become increasingly tired as the day progresses. Then, when they go to sleep at night, that drive steadily decreases until their brain and body are sure that they have slept sufficiently, at which point you wake up again. This process is guided by adenosine, a molecule in your cells. Adenosine builds up due to the use of your brain energy, causing your brain to function more slowly and your body to feel more tired as the day progresses. It probably makes sense to you now how your sleep drive contributes to the chronic insomnia issues that you experience; you are unable to sleep, so that adenosine never discharges, and you are left with a continually building supply of a molecule designed to tire you out.

That is not the entirety of what helps to regulate your sleep though. It is also important to have a healthy circadian rhythm cycle. This is the bodily process regarding sleep that most people are at least somewhat familiar with, because it is mentioned most often on TV and on social media, as well as in education. If you do not already know what this is, the circadian rhythm cycle is what makes sure that your body is synchronized to the 24-hour schedule our days run on (Suni, 2023). In a sense, this is also what is known as your body's internal clock.

Your circadian rhythm cycle is responsible for making sure that at various points of the day, your body is producing what it needs to and behaving how it should. In other words, the circadian rhythm cycles in your brain ensure that on a subconscious level, you know where morning, afternoon, and night tend to fall. This works based on the suprachiasmatic nucleus of your brain, where signals are sent to your body regarding what time it should be. The circadian rhythm cycle is why a lot of health experts recommend getting sunlight first thing in the morning; it is dictated by the day and night cycles we experience from changes in natural light. Circadian rhythm cycles are therefore incredibly easy to skew or rotate, because if you behave as though, for example, 7 p.m. is 7 a.m., soon your body will function as if that is truly how it is in real life.

The inability of the body to synchronize these two processes is a major contributor to many people's insomnia (The Drive to Sleep and Our Internal Clock | Healthy Sleep, 2007). If your body does not know when night and day are supposed to be, or you wake up at odd hours of the day, or even if you do not eat according to your body's natural circadian rhythm cycle, it can throw these two cycles off balance. Your body will not know what times it needs to release that adenosine, making you sleepy entirely too early or too late in the day, or maybe even not at all. Then you are unable to sleep at night because you napped earlier or because your body assumes you should go to sleep at some abnormal hour of the night.

Think about jet lag. When you fly into a different time zone, your body still functions on the clock of wherever you flew from, making it hard to fall asleep or stay awake in accordance with the time zone you currently live in. You can do the exact same thing without ever leaving the comfort of your home if you have unhealthy sleep habits. Sleep drive and circadian rhythm cycle desynchronization can result in anything from simple discomfort to something as severe as a sleep disorder, which includes narcolepsy and insomnia both. Learning how to manage your sleep schedule and patterns is necessary in order to ensure that these two processes remain synchronized.

Importance of Sleep

With that being said, it is incredibly important to ensure you have a healthy relationship with sleep. Sleeping enough each and every night is one of the most important things you can do for your health because it helps your body do everything at its best—without a proper night's sleep, your body lacks the strength and resources it needs to carry out various processes. The healthy impacts of sleeping both well enough and long enough extend to physical health and mental health alike.

Sleeping well makes physical activity easier, lowers your risk of heart disease and diabetes, and lowers inflammation while also strengthening your immune system (Leech, 2022). If you have suffered from insomnia for quite a while, once you regulate your sleep patterns it is almost certain that you will notice an improvement in various aspects of your mental health. On the mental side, sleeping enough makes your brain work faster, retain more information at a more accurate level and for longer durations, and reduces the symptoms of various mental illnesses like depression. It also increases your ability to socialize and process emotions in a meaningful way. It is clear that sleeping is vital to your health in more ways than one.

Stages of Sleep

It goes without saying based on the previous section that your body undergoes a wide variety of processes based on the time you sleep both before and after you rest, but what about what happens to your body while you are actively asleep? Understanding the different stages that your brain and body experience during sleep may help to highlight what kind of sleep you are missing out on as a result of your insomnia, which can be enlightening in determining which solutions in later chapters you should focus on the most.

Prior to 2007, it was thought that the sleep cycle consisted of five stages, but the American Academy of Sleep Medicine eventually consolidated that into just four stages instead (Cherry, 2007). These four stages are used to describe the activity of the brain and body as you fall asleep and throughout the duration of your rest. While you sleep, given that you are sleeping fully and restfully, your brain and body go through three NREM stages followed by one REM stage (Suni, 2021). The four stages of sleep in a normal, healthy sleep cycle are as follows:

- NREM Stage 1, also called N1. This stage typically lasts for 1-7 minutes and describes the stage of sleep when you first fall

asleep. At this stage, your brain and body begin to slow their processes down, but your body may not be relaxed yet. If you sleep uninterrupted throughout the night, as your body begins its natural repetition of these stages, you may spend less or even no time repeating N1 since your body will have been long relaxed by the second revolution through these stages.
- NREM Stage 2, also called N2. NREM Stage 2 typically lasts for 10-25 minutes. This describes the part of your sleep where your body temperature lowers, your muscles relax, and you begin to slow your breathing. Eye movement will slow to a stop, and your brain will begin to actively stop yourself from being interrupted from sleep. All of these changes are important to the process of falling asleep comfortably and being able to stay asleep, as if the body is unable to regulate itself in these ways you may wake up often or sleep uncomfortably.
- NREM Stage 3, also called N3, slow wave sleep, or deep sleep. NRED Stage 3 typically lasts 20-40 minutes, and during this stage your body is completely relaxed. At this stage of sleep, your brain releases something called delta waves, which are responsible for providing us with deep, restorative sleep. This is also thought to be the stage most important to physical health and memory, since delta waves have been noted to be incredibly beneficial to our brains.
- REM Sleep, lasting 10-60 minutes. While you are asleep, your brain activity rises to the level it usually is at while you are awake, and your body enters a state of near paralysis. The only processes that your body can carry out during REM sleep are breathing and movement of the eyes. Rapid eye movement during sleep is partially responsible for the ability to dream at night. It takes approximately an hour and a half to enter REM sleep, if not longer. As your brain repeats through these cycles, the amount of time you spend in REM sleep is greatest during the second half of your resting period.

It is important to know that sleep stages are not perfectly the same for everyone, every night, or even every cycle. Your body needs to experience six of these cycles each night to wake up feeling healthy and rested, and each time this cycle occurs the stages can be different and vary in length (Cleveland Clinic, 2021). For example, the first cycle may include all four stages and then the next cycle might be missing N1, and the third time you might spend way longer in REM sleep than in the previous two cycles. The sleep cycle and stages of sleep your body experiences during the night can be impacted by light, travel, work, physical or mental pain and stress, medication or substance use, and where you sleep (External Factors That Influence Sleep | Healthy Sleep, 2007), among other things.

Sleep Changes Across Your Lifespan

It is also completely normal for your sleep habits, cycles, and needs to change a little as you age. Your body undergoes a variety of changes throughout your lifetime, and your sleep related needs are no different. Each stage in your lifespan has the potential to alter the way you sleep, which means it is important to know roughly what your sleep cycle should look like at whatever age you may be.

The amount of sleep you need depends, above all, on your age. Newborn babies, for instance, tend to sleep at least 14 hours a night, whereas adults 65 and older need just 7-8 hours of sleep, the lowest of any age group (Suni, 2021). Teens usually need 8-11 hours of sleep, and those 18-64 will benefit most from 7-9 hours of sleep each night. The need for sleep seems to reduce as you age because of your brain aging and therefore different parts of it deteriorating over time. The suprachiasmatic nucleus I mentioned earlier, for example, deteriorates and results in your body needing less and less sleep based on how it affects your internal clock. Older individuals are less likely to experience restful sleep because of this as well as because of the changes in hormones older people experience. It is important to maximize the quality of your sleep as early as possible because of this.

Many people tend to be under the impression that you need less sleep as you age. In fact, many people studied for their sleep habits exhibit lower amounts of sleep the later in their life they get. While it may seem that because of this data you need less sleep, it is still healthy to try and sleep a relatively good amount every night no matter how old you get, preferably 8-9 hours. The reason people think that you need less sleep as you age is because your brain can function on lower levels of sleep due to lessened brain function. However, sleeping enough at night is a good way to slow the process of your brain aging in order to maintain function that some people lose due to sleeping less over time. Remember, though, that getting too much sleep is not a good thing either; aim for 8-9 hours of sleep consistently throughout adulthood whenever possible.

Sleep Quality vs. Sleep Quantity

I know how frustrating it can be to feel like no matter what you do or how much you sleep, you are never rested. You always wake up tired and feel like you could sleep for years no matter whether you just woke up from four hours of sleep or fourteen. You might even feel like you need to catch up on sleep that you missed the night before. What if I told you the amount you sleep isn't necessarily an important factor in how well you sleep at night? Believe it or not, many professionals believe the amount of time you sleep is reasonably less important than the overall quality of your sleep. A good night's sleep and a long night's sleep are two entirely different things—four hours of quality sleep can be so much more restorative and energizing than eight hours of low quality sleep. That is why learning the difference between sleep quantity and sleep quality can drastically change the game for you.

The quantity of your sleep can be impacted by the quality of your sleep and vice versa (Asp, 2020). The quantity of your sleep simply refers to the number of hours you have been asleep. So if you sleep for eight hours, then the quantity of your sleep is eight hours. Simple! The best way to ensure that you maintain a good sleep quantity is to find the lighting, temperature, and routines that work best for you. Later on, we'll cover how to find the optimal sleep environment to suit your needs in depth.

I mentioned that many professionals consider the quality of your sleep to be far more important than the number of hours you sleep. This is because many studies consistently seem to show that lower sleep quantity can be better for the brain and body than higher sleep quantity, if only the quality is optimized (Asp, 2020). Quality sleep, according to the National Sleep Foundation, is sleep that has the following characteristics:

- On average, each night you fall asleep in less than 30 minutes.
- You spend most of the time in bed asleep. You do not spend hours lying in bed for hours before or after you sleep.
- On any given night, it is expected that you will wake up at most one time during the night, and you will be able to go back to sleep easily if you do wake up that one time.

As someone who has suffered from insomnia speaking to someone else with insomnia, I know I've just given you a list of things you do not experience every or any night at all. That is one of the most frustrating parts of insomnia–the inability to meet all or any of the requirements of a restful night's sleep. Fortunately, it is possible to create habits that allow you to have a better sleep quality each night. Your sleep quality can be improved by refusing to use electronics 30-60 minutes before bedtime, going to sleep and waking up at the same time every day (yes, including weekends), limiting caffeine and alcohol consumption, and developing a bedtime routine (Asp, 2020). Bedtime routines to improve both sleep quality and quantity are a personal favorite of mine, because they are a great way to lower stress and prepare the mind and body for rest. It also gives you something to look forward to as part of your evening!

It is also important to know that even if sleep quality is a bit more important, you truly cannot rely solely on that to give you a good night's sleep. The perfect rest will be plentiful in quantity and quality.

Sleep Deprivation and Deficiency

There is also a difference between sleep deprivation and sleep deficiency, although you may be prone to use these terms interchangeably. For an adult, sleep deprivation simply refers to getting less than the seven to nine hours of sleep recommended for their age group (Suni, 2022). There are also multiple different types of sleep deprivation:

- Acute sleep deprivation, which is a short term form of sleep deprivation wherein someone sleeps far less than usual. Acute sleep deprivation usually lasts a week or less.
- Chronic sleep deprivation, which is sleep deprivation lasting at least three months where you fail to get "normal" levels of sleep regularly.
- Chronic sleep deficiency, which is a term describing chronic sleep deprivation that occurs alongside the inability to sleep uninterrupted or undisturbed.

Sleep deficiency, on the other hand, is what is medically referred to as insomnia and is a bit different from sleep deprivation. Sleep deficiency is far more broad than sleep deprivation, including not just failing to sleep enough, but sleeping at inappropriate times, sleeping poorly, or having a sleep disorder (National Heart, Lung, and Blood Institute, 2022). While sleep deprivation will make you exhausted the next day, sleep deficiency will lead to severe health problems as I mentioned earlier. It is possible to have both sleep deficiency and sleep deprivation, because sleep deprivation can be a symptom of sleep deficiency. The key difference is that sleep deprivation involves having too little time to sleep due to habitual actions, whereas sleep deficiency involves trouble sleeping even when you have ample time for it.

As you and I both know, sleep is a vital part of our daily lives. It is an essential component for us to maintain physical and mental health. Every night, our bodies need a certain amount of sleep in order to function properly throughout the day. Failure to get enough sleep and/or quality sleep can cause us to become easily tired, have difficulty concentrating, and so much more. If left unattended, serious health problems could arise from inadequate sleep. Unfortunately, insomnia is far too common and affects millions of people around the world.

Chapter 2:
Feels Like Insomnia

The American Sleep Association estimates that nearly 70 million Americans have a sleep disorder (Hull, 2021). That is over a fifth of the American population facing troubles sleeping at night. Insomnia remains the most prevalent of all the sleep disorders; about 30% of adults experience insomnia at some point in their life, and 10% of the population suffers from long-term insomnia. 10% might seem low at a glance, but let me put it this way: over 33 million of those Americans with sleep disorders suffer from long-term insomnia. If you feel like you might be in that 33 million, you could be right. Learning about the specifics of insomnia, its causes and treatments will be crucial in effectively combating it and removing you from that 10% of sufferers.

Overview of Insomnia

Insomnia is a sleep disorder that causes an inability to sleep sufficiently. It impacts both sleep quantity and sleep quality, and is a form of sleep deficiency. Those who suffer from insomnia feel the weight of being unable to wake up feeling rested and refreshed (Lamoreux & Raypole, 2022). Symptoms of insomnia include:

- Trouble falling asleep or staying asleep. Insomnia may lead to tossing and turning throughout the night, or waking up frequently throughout the night regardless of if you are interrupted or not.
- Worrying about falling asleep while trying to sleep, or tossing and turning at night, unable to fall asleep.
- A chronic inability to stay asleep; waking up multiple times or being easily interrupted from sleep and waking up feeling like you got no rest at all.

You might also be experiencing the symptoms of these symptoms, like fatigue or irritability. Insomnia is a disorder with a myriad of side effects and symptoms, and presents differently in everyone who has it. That does not at all minimize the amount of suffering faced by those who have insomnia. Even if you know that you experience insomnia, it can be frustrating to not know why you experience it. Therefore, next we'll discuss different theories and observed causes of insomnia.

Causes of Insomnia: The 3P Model

The first set of causes for insomnia I will touch on is the 3P model. Insomnia can be caused by a variety of interlacing factors, and the 3P model consolidates the three factors that sleep experts claim have the most impact on causing insomnia. In other words, the 3P model takes the thousands upon thousands of possible causes for insomnia and turns them into three overarching categories that assist in our ability to understand the causes that provoke the development or maintenance of insomnia. The 3P model for insomnia, developed by Arthur Spielman, asserts there are three main causes for insomnia, which he referred to as predisposition, precipitation, and perpetuation (Lefkowitz, 2020).

Predisposition is exactly what it sounds like: factors we are born with that place us at a greater risk for developing insomnia. Genetics can be a predisposing factor to your insomnia. If your parents have insomnia or anxiety, you are at a greater risk of developing insomnia or anxiety as well, which then can heighten insomniac tendencies. Predisposition is not something that can necessarily be cured, but it is something that individuals with predisposing factors contributing to insomnia can work to alleviate somewhat. Routines, strategies, and options I mention in later chapters can help reduce symptoms of insomnia faced even by those who experience sleep issues solely due to predisposition.

Precipitation in this case is not used to mean rain or weather. Instead, a precipitating factor when discussing insomnia is a trigger or a cause. Whatever triggered your first night rife with insomnia is your precipitating factor. This can be anything from a simple cold or illness to trauma or some other extreme change in your life. For mild triggers like a cold, you likely only experience short-term insomnia. This can usually be resolved far more easily in most cases. But for those of us who have trauma or other serious experiences to blame for insomnia, the cycle continues into the last P: perpetuation.

Perpetuation is anything you do to make your insomnia worse, consciously or not. Habits like doom scrolling on social media late after you have laid down to rest, drinking coffee to push yourself through the last hour of work, and taking naps throughout the day are all examples of things that can perpetuate insomnia. Perpetuation is the most difficult factor, because once you have developed those habits, they are very hard to break. Perpetuation is what causes most people to be trapped in an endless cycle of insomnia. One of the hardest things to admit for people suffering from any mental illness is that they play a role in perpetuating the symptoms of it, but once you find the ability to understand any potential role you play in worsening your insomnia, you can truly begin to work towards healing from it.

There is always the chance that your insomnia is not caused by you, a change, or predisposition. You could have a healthy family history and an absolutely perfect relationship with sleep, along with flawless routines most of us could envy, yet still suffer from insomnia. The 3P model does not explain away every single cause for insomnia, because there are several causes completely out of control.

Other Causes of Insomnia

It is possible to try and narrow the cause of your insomnia down more closely and realize it is completely outside of your control or something that can be easily fixed. The 3P model is effective at explaining how insomnia happens and progresses, but it does not clearly highlight the cause of your insomnia if it does not neatly fall into one of the three categories. The first thing to do is to rule out physical causes of insomnia. Being physically ill can prevent you from experiencing restful sleep, and it is not always obvious when you might be experiencing a physical illness. Some of these causes are highly unlikely, but it is always better to be safe. I encourage you to get yourself checked out by a doctor to rule out any physical causes of insomnia before you move forward with holistic treatment due to the variety of physical illnesses that can cause insomnia.

Mold intoxication, for example, can be very hard to detect but deadly if left untreated. For a lot of people, the symptoms of mold poisoning manifest just like a cold, flu, or even COVID. Mold is usually airborne, and it can grow behind your furniture, in your vents, or anywhere else that might see a lot of moisture (Suni, 2021). Ensuring your home is dehumidified properly is important because of this. Signs you may be experiencing mold intoxication include but are not limited to rashes, itchy eyes, sneezing, coughing, or blurred vision. More severe symptoms include fever, difficulty breathing, and lung infection. It is very important to treat and remove mold immediately, and to visit a doctor if you find mold in your home. The amount of mold does not matter; a very small amount can do drastic damage to your health and worsen your insomnia. If you think it is possible that you could have a mold infestation in your home, at home tests are relatively cheap online and hiring a professional to do an inspection is worth the comfort of knowing you are safe.

It is also possible that parasitic infection can disrupt your ability to sleep healthily. Parasites can go undetected for a long time, damaging your body all the while, and the ones that reside in your intestinal tract are most likely to cause insomnia (Carroll, 2018). Because parasites are no joke and are incredibly hard to detect without medical help, it is important to seek medical evaluation for your insomnia as soon as possible. More often than not, medical treatment early on can prevent the development of life shattering symptoms as a result of internal parasites.

Heavy metal poisoning is another scary yet possible cause for your insomnia. Heavy metal poisoning might seem like something you will never experience, but this is more common than you would think. Heavy metal poisoning can be contracted from mercury dental fillings, fish, tap water, drug usage, birth control, and many other sources (Lewis, 2022). Heavy metal poisoning is far less common nowadays, but it is not entirely impossible and therefore should not be disregarded entirely. If you eat a lot of fish, have a really old home that might've used lead paint or pipes, or suspect other causes for heavy metal poisoning, a trip to the doctors may be in order.

Adrenal fatigue and hyperglycemia are two other common causes for physically based insomnia, and both need to be diagnosed by a professional. Adrenal fatigue occurs when you become so stressed that your body can no longer keep up (Lam, 2016). When you face stress, your body produces cortisol to combat it. Adrenal fatigue is what happens when your body physically cannot produce sufficient levels of cortisol in order to handle the stress that you are facing. This can cause hypoglycemia, cravings for sweet or salty food, and general fatigue. Hyperglycemia is another cause for insomnia that can go undetected for a long time if you do not get regular medical check ups. It is more commonly referred to as diabetes or high blood sugar. This happens when the body does not have enough insulin or are unable to properly utilize the insulin it does have (Pacheco, 2022). Even if you think it is impossible for you to have diabetes, getting a second opinion from a medical professional is always best. If on the off chance you are diabetic and do not know, your doctor will guide you to the treatment you need to help your body feel the best it can and to alleviate your insomnia.

And finally, delayed sleep phase syndrome, or DSPS, is a cause of insomnia that many professionals are discovering is more common than it was previously thought to be. Delayed sleep phase syndrome is a type of circadian rhythm sleep disorder in which your body's internal clock is delayed by two or more hours (Nunez, 2019). This causes your body to fall asleep much later than what is considered to be socially acceptable, and DSPS is a lot more common than most people think. About 15% of the population has DSPS, with most of the sufferers being young adults or teenagers. This is not the same thing as being someone who prefers to be up late. For those with DSPS, you physically cannot sleep at an appropriate time even if you try your very best to do so. Many people with delayed sleep phase syndrome are unable to lead "normal" lifestyles due to the inability to entirely cure this disorder. Getting a professional opinion if you feel that you might be someone with delayed sleep phase syndrome is the best way to find out about solutions for moving forward and trying to develop a healthy relationship with sleep.

If you think there is even the slightest possibility that you could have any of these causes of insomnia, please do not hesitate to reach out to your doctor. If you do have one of these issues, medical help will alleviate your insomnia the fastest. Ruling out physical causes of insomnia that are out of your control will also let you know if you should proceed with some of the options I provide later on.

Types of Insomnia

Insomnia may seem cut and dry to you at first, but in actuality it is a multi-faceted disorder that comes in many different types. No one type of insomnia is the same. Chances are, if you know a lot of people who suffer from insomnia, you also know a lot of people who suffer from different types of insomnia as well. There are five main types of insomnia, and it can be very helpful to determine what type of insomnia you have so that you can appropriately treat that type (Radhakrishnan, 2022).

Acute insomnia is the type most people experience and is also the least severe form of insomnia. Typically, it lasts less than a month and is the product of changes in environment or stress levels. Acute insomnia can be caused by moving, temperature changes, a new job, or any other lifestyle change like that. Acute insomnia is easily treatable because it is both short-term and the least complicated form. Regularly, acute insomnia can resolve itself or can be resolved with minor aid.

Chronic insomnia is defined by experiencing insomnia for at least three nights a week for a month straight. This means that you experience the inability to fall asleep or stay asleep consistently for a month or longer. Professionals categorize chronic insomnia as either primary or secondary depending on the symptoms you face. Primary, or idiopathic insomnia, is insomnia with no specific cause. It is rare that insomnia has truly no connecting cause or trigger, so most people fall into the category of having secondary insomnia. Secondary insomnia, which is also referred to as comorbid insomnia, is insomnia that occurs as a result of some other medical condition. Physical or psychological conditions, medication, drug usage including nicotine and caffeine, age, stress, and chronic pain are all causes of chronic insomnia. It is not as difficult as it may seem to treat comorbid insomnia, because once you know which condition has triggered the insomnia, you can better move forward with a solution. Chronic insomnia can also be caused by onset insomnia.

Onset insomnia simply refers to the inability to fall asleep. This can be short or long-term and can cause anything from mood swings to depression and anxiety. Onset insomnia does not include any of the other symptoms of insomnia like being unable to stay asleep or struggling to sleep for sufficient amounts of time.

Maintenance insomnia is when someone experiences either a difficulty staying asleep or waking up too early with an inability to rest again. This is usually caused by other medical conditions like restless leg syndrome or acid reflux. This is different from comorbid insomnia in that maintenance insomnia specifies a symptom whereas comorbid insomnia refers to the duration of insomnia. It is possible to have more than one type of insomnia as well.

The last of the five types of insomnia is behavioral insomnia of childhood, which is caused by refusal or inability to sleep in a child. Habitually refusing to sleep as a child can set the stage for insomnia lasting in adulthood due to the brain never developing the habit of going to sleep regularly or at night. Fortunately, this type of insomnia can be treated easily in many different ways.

Treatment Options

Knowing the cause of your insomnia, or even having a reasonable suspicion as to the cause, is a great step forward. It is also a very validating experience for many people who suffer from insomnia. Though, once you learn the cause you might be struck with the realization that you do not know what is next. How do you move forward with treatment options? The American Academy of Sleep Medicine recommends two particularly strong candidates for curing insomnia: medication and cognitive behavioral therapy (CBT) (American Academy of Sleep Medicine, 2008).

Medication

Various medications are available for insomnia, both over the counter and prescription. Over the counter remedies for insomnia include things like melatonin, but for those who suffer from severe insomnia and want to take advantage of the option of medication as a treatment option, it may be best to visit a doctor to obtain a prescription. Doctors will often prescribe antidepressants, benzodiazepines, or other dedicated medications intended for helping patients sleep (WebMD Editorial Contributors, 2007). "Off label" prescription medications exist as well, such as hydroxyzine. Off label treatments are when doctors prescribe medications meant for something else to cure your symptoms. In the case of hydroxyzine, typically this medication is an antihistamine used for allergy relief. However, hydroxyzine has been seen to have effective impacts on patients with anxiety and insomnia, so doctors will often prescribe this in lieu of stronger medications at first. This might sound unsafe, but typically off label treatments are incredibly common and can even be safer. Off label prescriptions are often offered instead of stronger, more addictive medications, or because a significant number of patients with similar symptoms showed improvement in a way that was not necessarily expected from a certain medication. Make sure to express any concerns you have to your doctor before taking prescribed medication.

Taking medication to aid in sleep troubles can have various side effects, however, and you should be aware of them before opting to take medication for sleep. Sleep medications can cause oversleeping, difficulty concentrating, or drowsiness the next day (Suni, 2021). As a result, you should never start sleep medication if you have something important to do the next day, need to drive early in the morning, or anything else that could put you at risk of danger. Sleep medication can also cause an allergic reaction, so be sure that whatever prescription you receive does not contain something that you are allergic to. Pharmacists can usually tell you if any medication contains an ingredient, so be sure to ask them before you purchase your medication.

Unfortunately, as with any medication, sleep medication has the potential for dependence or addiction. Because of this, it is important to take the sleep medication exactly as prescribed and remember that sleep medication is not a permanent solution. Sleep medicines are only meant to be taken for a few weeks and in combination with positive lifestyle changes, so it is important to know this and avoid considering sleep medications to be a permanent solution to your insomnia. Doctors will most likely prescribe sleep medications for those who are struggling with a severely difficult lifestyle change or for those who cannot adapt to a new lifestyle sleep-wise.

It is also vital to know that you cannot simply stop taking medications like this when you feel like it. Stopping treatment with a medication can result in severe withdrawals and illness. It is important to wean yourself off these medications. A doctor will be able to provide the best advice to stop treatment. Some doctors, however, will insist that it is perfectly okay to stop taking a medication all at once. Even if this is true for some people, individually you may have a different experience. The best way to wean yourself off medicine is to slowly half your dose and lower that dose every few days. Do not cut medications that are not scored; instead, your doctor will usually be willing to provide a lower dosage if you notify them that you want to slow or stop treatment.

Finally, I want to stress that sleep medication is a temporary solution, a bandage for the symptoms of insomnia. Many doctors will not prescribe sleep medication long-term unless it is a more severe case because of the addictive nature of many prescriptions offered for sleep. Becoming dependent on a medication is never a good idea because of the physical and mental pitfalls of doing so. Dependency is a slippery slope and can lead to worsened insomnia over time, so be sure that while you are taking your medication you are also working on improving your insomnia in other ways. This will ensure that the impact of the medication is useful and that you develop long-lasting, healthy sleep habits.

Cognitive Behavioral Therapy

Cognitive behavioral therapy (CBT) has also been proven to be incredibly effective for insomnia. CBT is a short-term therapy aimed at identifying and changing thought patterns to be healthier or more objective instead of based on emotions, traumatic experiences, or bias (Bonomo, 2020). CBT is typically goal oriented, meaning that patients go into CBT with an idea of something they want to better, change, or accomplish as a result of their treatment. CBT has been proven to have a more long-term effect than medication because the goal of CBT is to provide its patients with lasting skills, resources, and coping mechanisms that can be carried throughout one's lifetime, even after they stop CBT treatment. I will discuss CBT more in depth in a later chapter.

If these treatment options seem slim, it is not quite time to worry just yet. The rest of this book will focus on holistic approaches that do not rely on medication to cure your insomnia. CBT is far more accessible than many people think at first, and I promise that you will appreciate some of the solutions offered moving forward.

My Story

It is at this point that I'd like to tell you a bit more about my personal journey with developing insomnia. My struggles with insomnia began during my time in high school. After months of stress and difficulties piling up, it all collapsed in on me. I struggled with balancing my schoolwork, social life, and other responsibilities, and my later interest in the night life did not help. The alcohol I consumed and the way I stayed up late at night contributed to the worsening of my insomnia. A stressful job change plagued me with feeling overwhelmed and unfulfilled at every turn. On top of that, my relationship with my long-term boyfriend came to a close at this point, and the health of one of my family members began to suffer catastrophically. I faced medical mishaps, trauma of all kinds, dependencies on sleep medication, and eventually lost my job after my drinking habits spiraled into alcoholism. I struggled with being a single mother and staying off of alcohol for the duration of my pregnancy before spiraling again afterwards.

During this period of my life, the days and eventually years passed by like a blur. Each day was brimming with exhaustion and stress. Anxiety overwhelmed my life and ate at me in the night, and no matter how hard I tried, I could not fall asleep at night. Eventually, I found the strength to decide that enough was enough and began to investigate treatment options that would work for me.

I want you to know a bit about my background because I want to make sure you know that no matter what you may be facing, you are not alone. There are so many people just like you out there, suffering from the torture that is insomnia on top of an already aggressive world that can sap the passion and motivation right out of us. By hearing my story, I hope that you will recognize how you deserve better than to be plagued by your insomnia, and that you will be inspired to work towards relieving yourself of its clutches. I want everyone to be able to experience the freedom I do now.

In this chapter, we covered essential insight into the causes, varieties, symptoms, and treatments of the condition that is insomnia. In the next chapter, I want to take you on a self-directed insomnia assessment. This is a valuable tool that will give you a much deeper understanding of your own insomnia triggers and what you can do to improve your overall sleep health, and we will use the results of this assessment in other parts of the book as well.

Chapter 3:
Check Yourself

"Knowing your weakness, is a strength" — *Dr Toyin Omofoye*

Before you can adequately approach finding a solution to your insomnia, you have to know your sleep-wake patterns. It can be a bit challenging to know where to start with evaluating your sleep patterns, which is why I've developed some helpful tips and tools for you to use in your journey. Self-evaluating those patterns via the assessment activities I include in this chapter will ensure you have a good understanding of your personal sleep patterns so that we can come to the best solution for your unique case of insomnia together.

Keep a Sleep Diary

One of the best ways to begin tracking your sleep patterns is to keep a sleep diary. A sleep diary is a place where you can record the times you went to sleep, when you woke up, every time you woke up during the night, the quality of your sleep, and anything else regarding how you slept so that it can be analyzed later (Troy, 2021). It is best to do this for at least two weeks, because a record of two full weeks is going to give you the best sample of how you typically sleep. You can keep a handwritten sleep diary or a digital copy, but because it is best to keep it near your bed, I personally recommend a paper and pen version. That way your sleep quality is not lowered by bringing screens into the equation.

A good template to use for filling out a sleep diary will include the following things (American Psychological Association, 2023):

- At approximately what time did you get in bed?
- At approximately what time did you begin the process of trying to fall asleep?

- Approximately how long did it take to fall asleep after you began trying to sleep?
- How many times did you wake up for the night, not counting when you officially woke up for the day?
- How long did you stay awake during the periods you woke up throughout the night, and what did you spend your time doing during those periods?
- What time did you officially wake up?
- What time did you physically get out of bed?
- How well did you sleep?

It is essential that you do not use a sleep diary as an excuse to watch the clock like a hawk. Just make your best guess about what times each thing occurred and the duration of it; clock watching is a good way to worsen the effects of your insomnia and provide you with an incredibly inaccurate sleep diary. The purpose of your sleep diary is to track and analyze your sleep patterns, but that does not mean it has to be accurate down to the minute. It should be a record of your natural sleep patterns, and even estimates are valuable because they provide an opportunity to analyze your perceptions of time relating to sleep. Sleep diaries can also be an effective tool to examine with a doctor if you seek one out to help you determine possible treatment options, as having a pre-filled sleep diary will give your doctor some statistics to work with initially.

For a more effective sleep diary, keeping track of your sleep pattern for at least two weeks before you begin seeking insomnia solutions is best. Two weeks provides you with enough data to know your typical sleep patterns, because you are unable to rely on just a night or two to understand how you usually sleep. Once you have recorded this data, you can keep using your sleep diary while you seek solutions in order to monitor your progress. I recommend adding in sections for changes you have made and how they impacted your sleep so that you can determine which things did and did not work for improving your sleep patterns.

Determine Disruptors

Now that you have your sleep diary set up, it would be a good idea to include a space to record the various disruptors that play a role in your insomnia. This can be in the same journal or a different one as you use to record your sleep patterns. Personally, I think that it is best to include all of the data in the same journal, dedicating a page per night in order to have all of the information you need in one place for easy reference.

A sleep disruptor is anything that contributes to a poor night's sleep by means of shortening or interrupting your sleep (Terry, n.d.). Anything that causes you to fall asleep late, wake up early, wake up often, or fail to fall into a state of deep sleep is considered to be a sleep disruptor. Sleep disruptors fall within three common categories: behaviors, thoughts, and environment.

Behaviors as a sleep disruptor include habits you engage with throughout the day that contribute to sleeping poorly at night. I mentioned developing a bedtime routine a bit earlier, and that is because the way you spend your evening just before you lay down to sleep can have a tremendous impact on the quality of rest you have that night. There are many bad habits that most people with insomnia engage in that can prove detrimental to their sleep. At least one of the following likely applies to you:

- Using electronics before bed. Watching TV or scrolling through social media is often a wonderful way to ensure you have incredibly poor sleep (Chambers, 2020). This is because screens emit blue light that prevents our brain from releasing melatonin, the chemical that puts us to sleep.
- Eating heavy foods or drinking caffeine before bed. Ideally, you should be eating dinner early enough that it can be digested before bedtime. Heavy, undigested meals do not make for a restful night's sleep. It is also a bad idea to drink caffeinated drinks six or less hours before bed.
- Sleeping in a room with inadequate lighting or temperatures. The darker and quieter the room the better, and the ideal sleep temperatures are between 60 and 67 degrees (Chambers, 2020).

It is necessary to prevent light from entering the room as this can disrupt your sleep by alerting your eyes to daylight, and a room that's too warm will prevent your body from cooling to the optimal temperature for sleep.
- Lying in the bed for reasons other than sleep. People usually sleep best when their brain associates the bed solely with sleeping. If you work, relax, or study in your bed, you are effectively eliminating the connection between your bed and sleeping in your brain.
- Sleeping at different times each night, and/or waking up at different times. If you go to bed and wake up at the same time each day, it programs your brain to associate those times with the appropriate sleep cycle stages. By switching up your sleep-wake patterns intentionally, you confuse your brain's sleep schedule and circadian rhythm cycles, causing your brain to make inappropriate or contradictory decisions about when to wake or sleep.

The mindset and thoughts you have can also be disruptors to your sleep health. For example, negative beliefs about sleep can cause insomnia, while positive or realistic outlooks on sleep have been linked to improvements in sleep health in those who have sought treatment for insomnia (Carey et al., 2010). According to some research, developing unhealthy or counterproductive beliefs about your sleep pattern can then transfer into stress or anxiety that prevents you from sleeping (Ong et al., 2012). In other words, if your brain is brimming with thoughts that you will never fall asleep or get enough sleep, it will cause you to stress out and be unable to sleep because of that stress. Other negative thoughts that can harm your sleep are making negative or unrealistic assumptions about sleep, blaming everything bad in your life on insomnia, and overall spending hours of your time ruminating on negative aspects of sleep (Centre for Clinical Interventions, n.d.).

Sleep Beliefs Assessments are a common tool used to analyze your general attitudes towards sleep and anything associated with it. Instead of providing you with one that is pre-made, I have developed a unique Sleep Beliefs Assessment for you to take. The questions below are gathered from a variety of other assessments and current research regarding insomnia. For each statement below, rate each statement 1-

10 depending on the extent to which you agree with it. You can feel free to jot your responses down on paper if you need to record them, or in the margins if you have a physical copy of the book. Rating a statement with a one represents completely disagreeing with the statement, and a ten represents agreeing entirely. Consider each statement genuinely and carefully, and rate each one based on your current, actual feelings regarding the statement.

1. If I do not get eight hours of sleep, I will not feel refreshed the next day.
2. I do not need as much sleep because I am aging.
3. If I am unable to fall asleep or wake up and cannot go back to sleep, I should stay in bed and try harder to fall asleep.
4. I am afraid I might die in my sleep, or that something bad will happen to me.
5. If I have a bad day, it is usually because I did not sleep very well the night before.
6. It is better to take a sleeping pill to knock myself out than risk even one bad night of sleep.
7. My insomnia rules my life to the point that I cannot enjoy hobbies or relationships because of it.
8. Insomnia is entirely a mental issue.
9. My sleep patterns will never get better, and I will be an insomniac for life.
10. Other people can fall asleep at will, so I should be able to too.
11. Other people can drink caffeine and fall right asleep, so I should be able to as well.
12. If I get a bad night of sleep, I know I will not be able to enjoy anything the next day.
13. I often cancel plans because I slept poorly the night before.
14. There is nothing I can do to improve my insomnia.
15. I am more rested by spending more time in bed, no matter what.
16. I need to "catch up" on my sleep that I missed by sleeping more the next day.
17. Just because I took a nap does not mean I should be unable to sleep at night too.
18. The food I eat does not matter with regards to my sleep.
19. One bad night of sleep means I'll surely sleep terribly for the next few days to come.

29

20. I have no control over my ability to sleep.

Add all of your scores up, and divide the number by 20. For example, if your scores for each question add up to 93, divide that by 20 and you will get 4.65. If your score is greater than or equal to four, as is the example score I just provided, then you likely have thoughts that deter healthy sleep patterns. Noticing you do have unhealthy sleep beliefs at this point is not a bad thing–it gives you a clear reference point for attitudes you need to work on in order to optimize your sleep.

Finally, the third major sleep disruptor is sleep environment. Your sleep environment is your bedroom, and there are certain standards that need to be met to have a relaxing sleep environment that is conducive to good sleep. Elements to mind regarding your sleep environment include temperature, noise, lighting, and your bedding. A good sleep environment is one free of noise, light, and heat, and your mattress should be right for your body. It is entirely possible to sleep poorly because of a mattress that is too soft or too hard.

In order to ensure that your sleep environment is perfect for rest, it should meet the following requirements:

- Quiet or silent. Any noise should be non-distracting, such as white or brown noise or ambient noise if you require sound to sleep.
- No lights, or a sleep mask should be worn. If you absolutely need a bit of lighting in the room, using low lighting such as a night light or a salt lamp is ideal.
- The temperature of the room is in the 60s. I personally prefer my room to be 66 or 67 degrees.
- Your bed is the right hardness level, and your bedding is clean and soft. If your bed is too uncomfortable because it is too soft or too hard, it may be time to find a new mattress.

As an optional inclusion, if you find pleasure in nice scents to help you relax, something lightly scented involved in your bedding or by your nightstand is a fabulous way to improve your sleep habits and attitudes. If you have other inclusions that are non-disruptive and that you are sure will improve the quality of your sleep at night, feel free to make adjustments as needed—it's your sleep environment after all!

In this chapter, we discussed your sleep patterns as well as potential factors that prevent you from sleeping well. You have taken an assessment that keys you in on which sleep beliefs you have that are unhealthy or prohibit you from getting a good night's sleep. Next, we're going to look at the first option for treatment, which focuses on healing the mind.

Chapter 4:
Cognitive Behavioral Therapy for Insomnia

"The soul always knows what to do to heal itself. The challenge is to silence the mind" — Caroline Myss

Cognitive Behavioral Therapy, also referred to as CBT, is a psychological treatment wherein a therapist guides you through the process of changing your thinking patterns from unhealthy ones that are holding you back in some way into thought patterns that are constructive and beneficial (American Psychological Association, 2017). This can include learning to identify unhealthy thought patterns, understand the thoughts and motivations of others, how to solve problems constructively, and more.

According to the American Psychological Association, there are three principles upon which CBT bases its methods. The first is that psychological problems are partially caused by faulty thinking. Faulty thinking creates distortions or inaccurate beliefs about the world around you, which in turn contribute to unhealthy habits or behaviors based on those poorly developed thought patterns. Eliminating faulty thinking is a key goal of CBT. The second principle of CBT is that psychological problems are partially caused by learned, unhelpful behavior. The way you were raised or the routines that are familiar to you may seem comforting or difficult to break, but in all reality a lot of those behaviors can be holding you and the quality of your sleep back. CBT works to analyze those behaviors and redirect them into behaviors that are more beneficial to you. And the third and final principle of CBT is that people with psychological issues are able to learn to cope with those problems in order to better their lives. This is a very uplifting aspect of CBT; no psychological issue is left in the dust with this treatment option because it encourages and promotes healing and coping skills that actually work.

CBT has been proven to have a plethora of benefits for those who spend time with it and genuinely try to reap those benefits. Those who have dedicated time to working with a CBT approach have noticed healthier thoughts, behaviors, and feelings (Cherry, 2022) regarding the various issues that incited them to enter CBT treatment. CBT is also a good option for those seeking short term therapy, because the benefits can be observed after just five sessions for many clients. This means after a few sessions of CBT, you will learn most if not all of the skills you will need to cope with your problem that brought you to treatment. After that, it is up to you to implement those tools in your own life. CBT is also one of the cheaper options available and is effective both in person and via telehealth. Telehealth is also typically more affordable for clients than in person therapy, and it is much easier to find bookings online. CBT patients learn to manage an array of mental illnesses and power through various struggles in their life in a way that provides them with skills that can be utilized for the duration of their lifetime, making CBT a powerful option for improving mental health. CBT has also notably been beneficial in decreasing the symptoms of insomnia, which is why I recommend it as one of the three pillars of insomnia cures.

Cognitive Behavioral Therapy for Insomnia

Myself and thousands of others have had amazing experiences with the effects of CBT on our insomnia. CBT specifically aimed to target insomnia is referred to as CBT-I, and focuses on three main factors that allow insomnia to continue in one's life (*Procedures*, n.d.). CBT-I focuses on things interrupting your sleep, the behaviors and habits that you frequent which contribute to perpetuating your insomnia, and reducing mindsets that contribute to your insomnia. This means that CBT-I is effectively a tool that works to eliminate patterns and behaviors that you know you do actively, determine factors that you are not aware contribute to your unhealthy sleep, and works to make you feel more positively towards yourself and how you sleep. This is especially good for those who scored high on the Sleep Behavior Assessment in chapter three, because the CBT-I approach helps eliminate a myriad of those harmful thoughts. For many sufferers of insomnia, those thoughts are a significant contributor to the inability to sleep, and you know this well if you are someone who spends a lot of time awake entangled in thought.

CBT-I is often thought by researchers to be the best and most effective treatment for severe and long-term insomnia for those hoping to do so without the use of medication (Rossman, 2019). In fact, the strategies taught during CBT-I have been noted to produce equivalent or better effects compared to medication for sleep, and have none of the negative side effects connected to medications. Insomnia oriented CBT also maximizes long term improvements related to insomnia and minimizes the potential to relapse into insomnia related behaviors and attitudes. This is because instead of providing a temporary bandage to your issues, CBT-I actually addresses the root causes and situations that worsen insomnia which leads to lifelong skill sets you can employ to alleviate insomnia. Anyone looking to resolve the harsh woes of insomnia in a short, unmedicated period of time can look to CBT as a first line of defense, and I actually encourage you to do so. Unlike medicine, CBT-I produces results that actually last because it targets the causes of insomnia instead of the symptoms.

There are five key components of CBT-I (*Procedures*, n.d.).

Sleep consolidation or restriction, which focuses on providing patients with skills needed to sleep in one stage instead of napping throughout the day, or teaches other habits tailored to improve sleep habits in clients.
Stimulus control, which focuses on controlling the various stimuli noted to create poor sleep habits or environments.
Cognitive restructuring, or changing your mindset regarding negative thoughts about sleep.
Sleep hygiene, which will be discussed in a later chapter.
Relaxation techniques, which will also be covered later on too.

Since this chapter focuses on providing foundational knowledge of CBT-I, in later chapters, I will describe the components of CBT-I in more detail.

The most reputable place to seek CBT-I treatment is from licensed professionals like doctors, therapists, or psychiatrists, and there are even professionals who specialize in CBT-I that you can search for both online and in person(Newsom, 2020). If there is not a professional readily available in your area, that is nothing to worry about and is the common experience of many seeking out a CBT-I psychiatrist. CBT-I is in incredibly high demand because of how well it works, but do not worry–CBT-I is equally as effective via telehealth or group therapy, and there are even self-guided formats that you can coach yourself through.

One of my goals through the next few chapters of this book is to empower you to employ CBT-I skills yourself, whether you plan to seek professional help or not. It might feel to you now that self-guided therapy is a fruitless venture and that you NEED a professional to guide you through it, but I promise that is not true in the case of CBT-I and various other forms of therapy. Self-guided therapy can be incredibly powerful and effective, especially regarding your insomnia healing journey. Various studies have noted that self-guided therapy has shown significant reductions in anxiety and depression, and the data also supports that these benefits endured years later (Drevitch, 2016). There is little to no data to support that self-guided CBT-I therapy is more harmful than good, so trying it out yourself is the best way to determine if you truly need professional intervention. And at the end of the day, you know yourself best and you spend the most time with yourself, so who better to guide you through this process than you?

If you are still unsure, some definitive signs that self-guided CBT-I may be for you are (Self-Guided Therapy, n.d.):

- You need access to low-cost treatment options, do not have access to insurance, or are otherwise financially not in a position to pay for medical treatment through a professional.
- You want to get started quickly and understand that appointments may slow down the therapeutic process.
- You are struggling to find licensed practitioners in your area and/or feel that appointments via telehealth are too impersonal for you.
- You have a busy schedule or need access to remote options that are more flexible.

- You are uncomfortable with the idea of therapy as of right now and want to try healing on your own before seeking professional intervention.
- You are self-aware and enjoy working towards self improvement.

If any of these fit your situation, self-guided CBT-I is absolutely a good place to get started with healing your mind from insomnia. You can find resources for self-guided CBT-I for free online incredibly easily, because CBT-I is both easy and in such high demand. The reason that so many people are unfamiliar with CBT-I or do not seek it out is because they are unaware of just how easy those resources are to access yourself. You can find articles, videos, workbooks, and more with a simple Google search. Oh, and I will go into more depth with how to guide yourself through CBT-I in the next few chapters—I promise the process is really simple.

Regardless of which method you choose for CBT-I, it is a good idea to give the methods and practices involved a shot at curing your insomnia, especially if you scored high on the Sleep Beliefs Assessment that you took earlier on.

My Story

The reason that I can personally advocate so strongly for the benefits of CBT-I is that the process was truly a game changer for my insomnia. Without the benefits and strategies I gained from CBT-I, I do not know if I would be where I am today in my journey.

As I mentioned in my last excerpt, I had been struggling for years with insomnia and it began to take a major toll on my life. I was exhausted all day every day, could not focus on my work no matter how hard I tried, and found myself to be increasingly frustrated and irritable.

My doctors seemed puzzled; they were unable to come to a sound diagnosis explaining my insomnia, so I reasoned that it was time to try something new. I was skeptical that CBT would be for me, but almost immediately after beginning my treatment, my evenings granted me immense relaxation. My CBT therapist offered me various exercises to calm my mind, and they actually worked. My anxiety about sleeping practically dissolved.

My therapist was also able to target mental patterns and unhealthy thought processes that disrupted my ability to sleep well. I became able to change these processes as well and found all of the anxiety I faced at night melting away with each session. Over time, I found myself more able to drift into a smooth, restful sleep as a result of the things I learned during CBT-I.

The benefits I experienced are undeniable, and I want to ensure that you know every option available to you. CBT-I, self-guided or not, is a sure-fire way to improve at least some of the symptoms of your insomnia. It is a process well worth trying.

Chapter 5:
Restrict and Control

> *"There is a time for many words, and there is also a time for sleep."*
>
> — *Homer, The Odyssey*

After developing a baseline understanding of how CBT-I works, I am going to guide you through two of the main components of the practice. This will allow you to begin to implement skills taught in CBT-I in a self-guided way, saving you time and money involved in the process of therapy. Even if you plan to seek out professional assistance in your CBT-I journey, trying methods on your own will provide your therapist with a good starting point for what does and does not work for you. The two powerful strategies we are going to focus on are sleep restriction and stimulus control.

Sleep Restriction

The first skill that I am going to teach you is sleep restriction. I know, that sounds counterintuitive. As someone suffering from insomnia, I know you already feel like your sleep is incredibly restricted as is. But sleep restriction as a method for curing insomnia is not at all what it sounds like. Instead of sleep depriving yourself, sleep restriction focuses on providing you with guidelines for developing healthy sleep patterns.

Sleep restriction as a method of improving insomnia related symptoms focuses on limiting the amount of time you spend in bed (Robards, 2022). This limits the time you are in bed based on your overall average time in bed in order to concentrate your rest periods and make them more productive. In other words, if you typically only get five hours of sleep but spend seven in bed just lying there, sleep restriction encourages you to only spend five hours in bed. Following this method is a wonderful way to increase your sleep efficiency, because once you have mastered this skill, you will be spending most of the time in bed actually sleeping instead of tossing and turning or waking up often throughout the night.

The goal of sleep restriction has nothing to do with cutting back on actual sleeping; sleep restriction makes it so that you have less of an imbalance between time spent in bed and time spent asleep. Sleep restriction practices therefore work to condition your brain to associate the bed with actually sleeping instead of lying awake anxiously hoping to pass out. It also works to program your brain to associate a certain schedule with sleeping so that you maintain a consistent sleep schedule. Because of the method involved in implementing sleep restriction, it can take several weeks to actually reap the benefits of sleep restriction (Rosenberg, 2020). Do not be discouraged by this, though. The gradual process of experiencing benefits slowly is known to ensure those benefits are long lasting and will not disappear once you stop consciously engaging in sleep restriction.

Sleep restriction works best for those experiencing insomnia and related symptoms due to disruptive behaviors. For those who suffer from insomnia due to mental or physical health issues, sleep restriction may not be an effective solution to your insomnia. It will not hurt to try it anyway, but there are methods guaranteed to work far better for your particular situation. If you suffer from a combination of illness and disruptive behavior, it is entirely possible that sleep restriction can alleviate at least some of your symptoms. Please note that this method is not effective if you suffer from the inability to stay awake during the day, and attempting to implement sleep restriction if that is your primary issue with sleep will not be beneficial to your overall sleep health (Kaiser Permanente, n.d.). At the end of the day, the decision is your own and it is ultimately up to you if you think sleep restriction is a helpful method to give a chance to improve your ability to sleep.

Guidelines and Implementation

There is a right way and a wrong way to implement sleep restriction. Those who know the right way to do so are the ones who are going to appreciate the benefits of a sleep restriction practice. Here is the RIGHT way to employ sleep restriction to your benefit (Kaiser Permanente, n.d.):

1. Determine how long you are allowed to spend in bed every night. The professional recommendation is that you start with five to five and a half hours, even if you sleep much less than this, if you work or have other responsibilities that you handle daily. Starting with less than five hours can result in more exhaustion than you started with. Otherwise, the ideal starting place is the amount of time that you spend asleep plus 30 minutes. So if you spend six hours asleep at night, start with a limit of 6.5 hours.
2. Select a specific time in the morning that works best for you. You will need to wake up at the same time each morning no matter what.
3. Determine what time you will go to bed. This should be based on the data from steps one and two. For example, if you need to be awake at seven each morning, 7 a.m. minus 6.5 hours is 12:30 a.m. This means you need to go to bed at 12:30 a.m. every single night.
4. Follow this routine for two weeks to the best of your ability for the best results. After two weeks, if you find yourself sleeping well on this schedule but feel that you need more sleep because you are tired during the day, you can add 15 more minutes to your time in bed. This should affect your bedtime, not your wake up time. Increase your time in bed by 15 minutes per week as needed until you find what works best for you.

This technique might be a bit difficult to manage at first, especially if you are relatively used to a tumultuous sleep routine. If you start feeling more tired than normal after about a week, that is, believe it or not, a good thing. This means your body is adjusting to your new schedule, and eventually you will find more success sleeping at night.

Sleep Restriction Tips

There are tons of things you can do in addition to the above that will help you experience more success with sleep restriction. For instance, it is a good idea to avoid napping at all costs. You should only be asleep during the hours you have given yourself each night. You should also only be in your bed during those hours as well. If you frequently relax in bed or work in bed, dedicate a different space in your home for these tasks. A desk, the couch, or a comfortable chair is more suited to these tasks and will allow your brain to recognize the bed as a spot solely for restful sleep when you get into bed.

It is also beneficial to use light to your advantage and to make your bedroom a place you enjoy. Bright lights such as window lights and overhead lights are optimal for mornings, but in the evening treating your brain to a cozy evening lamp light or candlelight will get you in the swing of feeling more tired at night. You can further amplify your bedtime routine by making your bedroom comfortable and cozy; use clean, comfortable bedding, pillows you like, and set the room to an ideal temperature. It is best if you make winding down for the evening something you enjoy doing, so find ways to embrace your routine. Reading a book, working on a puzzle or other crafts, light stretching, meditation, and caffeine free tea are all good ways to treat your body and mind at bedtime, and all of these activities are sure to help you rest better. Remember not to do anything harsh or extensive just before bed—we want to focus on soothing and calming the mind.

Stimulus Control

The other technique that we are going to cover in this chapter is stimulus control as a cure for insomnia. But first, we need to learn a little bit about classical conditioning. Classical conditioning is a psychological concept that describes a process by which learning occurs subconsciously (Elmer, 2020). You might have heard of this concept in school or be vaguely familiar with it if you have ever heard of the Pavlov's Dog experiment. Essentially, classical conditioning trains your brain to react a certain way to a certain light, sound, noise, pattern, or anything else, in a specified way. You will not necessarily ever think about the connection, but your brain makes it anyway.

A basic background on classical conditioning is important for understanding stimulus control for insomnia. For stimulus control, you will effectively be conditioning yourself to respond to an external cue like your bed as a signal to go to sleep (Stimulus Control, n.d.). This works by allowing your brain to form an association between your sleep environment and sleeping. You likely already experience a form of sleep-related classical conditioning and do not know it. If you find yourself watching TV, eating meals, working, studying, or otherwise spending copious amounts of time in bed, you have successfully and effectively conditioned your brain to stay awake in the presence of your bed–this has turned your bed into a place that elicits the same response that a living room or office would.

In order to correct this, it is necessary that you work to redirect and condition your brain to respond to the bed with tiredness. This is what the bedroom does in the minds of those with healthy sleep patterns; they see the bed and are conditioned to want to go to sleep. Psychologically, these individuals consider the bed to be a place of rest and relaxation, and therefore are able to sleep healthily. They don't see the bed as a place for hobbies, work, studying, or dinner, and instead find other places in the house for those activities, thus preserving the bed solely for sleep and sleep-related activities. For people with chronic, behavior-induced insomnia, the bed can trigger their brains in the exact opposite way. The bed can be a source of wakefulness if you are used to spending your whole day in bed doing things that require some level of alertness. That is why, when using stimulus control, it is important to connect the environment of your bedroom to the feelings of relaxation and preparing to sleep, then actually falling asleep later on.

Rationale and Implementation

There are several rules to follow when implementing stimulus control for insomnia, and they are as follows (Bootzin & Perlis, 2011):
1. Only get in the bed to go to sleep.
2. Only get in the bed to go to sleep when you actually feel tired. This helps you to become more aware of how your body feels when it is ready to go to sleep, which is far more intuitive than getting in bed because you "need" to.
3. Do not do anything besides sleep or relevant sexual activity in your bed. This means no TV, no Netflix, no YouTube, no

worrying, no eating, no anything else in bed. This rule allows you to form a connection between the bed and sleep.
4. If you get in bed and are unable to sleep, go to a different room. Only return once you think you can go to sleep again. Do not go out of your way to watch the clock, but aim to get up after 10 minutes of lying awake in bed. Repeat this step as needed.
5. Get up at the same time each morning. This will regulate your sleep patterns.
6. Do not take naps. Doing so will prevent you from getting a restful night of sleep.

Minor modifications can be made to the above rules as needed, especially if you are doing this while engaging with the aforementioned sleep restriction technique. For example, you can read in your bedroom if that is part of your winding down or nighttime routine, but you should not make it a habit to read as a hobby in bed. You should never break steps 5 or 6.

Now that we have covered sleep restriction and stimulus control for aiding in relieving insomnia, we are going to move onto another set of CBT-I techniques: cognitive distortions and cognitive restructuring. These are invaluable tools when managing your insomnia.

Chapter 6:
Question Your Mind

"Watch your thoughts, they become your words; watch your words, they become your actions; watch your actions, they become your habits; watch your habits, they become your character; watch your character, it becomes your destiny." –Lao Tzu

Cognitive Distortions & Impact on Sleep

A cognitive distortion is a negative thinking pattern that has no basis factually. These are thought patterns that emphasize negative biases and are typically used as a coping mechanism (Stanborough, 2019). An example of a cognitive distortion you might have said yourself at some point in your life is "Because I have failed, I am no good at this and I should never try it again." Cognitive distortions are called distortions because they display reality in a way that is false. Failure does not mean that you should give up, and rationally people who use that distortion know that somewhere in their mind. The reality of the universe is not that failure indicates you should never do something, and the cognitive distortion inaccurately represents that truth in an unproductive way. This, then, leads to holding yourself back, stress and anxiety, and missed opportunities.

There are many different types of cognitive distortions, all of which have the potential to impact your ability to have a good night's sleep. Because cognitive distortions have the tendency to provide you with an unrealistic view of your reality, they can cause significant difficulty in your ability to get to sleep. Take a look and see if you can identify the role any of these cognitive distortions play in your life, regarding sleep or otherwise:

- Labeling: giving yourself, an activity, or a concept a negative label as a result of an outcome you did not prefer.

- Emotional reasoning: believing that your emotions are more true than factual evidence.
- "Should": Believing that you "should" have done something or "should" be able to do something in a given situation.
- Discounting the positive: Dismissing positive events in favor of emphasizing negative ones, or contributing the positives in your life to coincidence and the negatives as reality.
- Mind reading: Trying to assume the thoughts or feelings of others.
- Personalization: Taking everything as a personal slight, fault, or a responsibility.
- Catastrophizing: Assuming the worst with no evidence.

At least a few of those cognitive distortions are probably really familiar to you. Studies show that those who have insomnia tend to show signs of a myriad of these cognitive distortions, which can worsen your insomnia (Gupta, 2016). Giving into these cognitive distortions regarding sleep can be a result of anxiety about how hard it is to fall asleep. This can build up and contribute to you distorting reality about sleep. One bad night of sleep can quickly distort into the belief that every night will be a bad night for you, which is one of the most common cognitive distortions about sleep (Felix, 2020). Thoughts like this are not always true, and believing that they are without evidence can make you anxious and struggle to sleep even more.

If you suffer from insomnia related cognitive distortions, all hope is not lost. Through cognitive restructuring, a common strategy learned in CBT-I, you can learn to take the power away from these distortions. Once you have developed the ability to remove power from the distortions, you will be able to enjoy a far better quality of sleep.

Cognitive Restructuring

Cognitive restructuring is the process through which unhealthy mindsets, including cognitive distortions, are identified and reframed so that they are replaced with healthy thought patterns (Stanborough,

2020). This is done by identifying and deconstructing unhealthy thought patterns. These thoughts are rationalized, and patients who undergo CBT based cognitive restructuring are taught how to have a more balanced outlook on the same scenarios. Cognitive restructuring works assuming that if you can change your mindset, you can change your emotions and actions to match. With regard to CBT-I specifically, cognitive restructuring is intended to identify unhealthy thoughts surrounding sleep and transform them into more positive attitudes, therefore working to alleviate symptoms of insomnia resulting from hindering thoughts.

Implementation

Cognitive restructuring can be done either with a therapist or other professional or through self-guided CBT practice. If you are hoping to implement cognitive restructuring on your own, here are some helpful steps you can take:

1. Identify negative or hindering beliefs that you have about sleep. If you do not feel confident about where to start, revisit your Sleep Beliefs Assessment from chapter three, and highlight each question you scored more than a three on.
2. Choose one negative belief from the list of beliefs you hold regarding sleep. Eventually, you can work on tackling all harmful beliefs, but for now it is best to start with one to create a gradual change.
3. Consider alternative viewpoints about the belief. For example, think about what would happen if you did not hold this belief, whether there is evidence supporting or contradicting your belief, if your belief places the blame for a situation elsewhere, the most realistic worst-case scenario, and advice you would offer to a friend in the same situation.
4. Come up with an alternative belief that provides you with a more positive outlook on the situation.
5. When you find yourself lapsing into that negative belief, remind yourself of all the reasons you listed in step three explaining why that belief may be invalid.

An example of working through cognitive restructuring a belief could look like the following:

A negative belief I have is that if I sleep badly tonight, my day tomorrow cannot be good.
I have identified the belief I will tackle above.
If I did not believe that this was true, I might have a more positive day tomorrow because I will not be dwelling on the negative night before. Thinking that I will have a bad day places the blame on my sleep instead of all of the other bad factors that could cause a bad day, and does not give any credit to the good that can happen. If my friend had this same problem, I would tell her to try and relax anyway and find something to look forward to tomorrow even if she felt her day was going poorly.
My new belief: If I sleep badly tonight, I can still have a good day tomorrow!

Challenge Common Negative Sleep Beliefs

An important aspect of working to better your mindset regarding sleep is to challenge negative beliefs about sleep. Negative beliefs about sleep don't just give you a reason to toss and turn at night; they also increase stress and anxiety which on their own are major contributors to the worsening of insomnia. To better help you work on cognitive restructuring, I am going to provide you with 10 of the most common negative beliefs about sleep, and then give you 10 examples of positive thoughts you could replace those negative beliefs with.

The top 10 negative beliefs about sleep are as follows (Session 3 Cognitive Restructuring and Sleep Medication Reduction Techniques, n.d.):

- "I will never fall asleep."
- "I woke up in the middle of the night and am wide awake, so I will not be able to fall back asleep."
- "I will not be able to function tomorrow."
- "I have to get eight hours of sleep."
- "I am unable to fall asleep unless I take a sleep pill."

- "My insomnia is going to cause health problems."
- "I feel awful due to my insomnia."
- "I will never be able to sleep better."
- "I did not get any rest at all last night."
- "There must be something wrong with me."

If you recognize that these are thoughts about sleep you have often, instead, try to restructure your brain to think of the same ideas like this:

- "I will be able to fall asleep when my body is relaxed and ready."
- "I will probably be tired again soon, but if not, that means I got enough rest for tonight."
- "The worst that can happen is I will be a bit tired. I will feel better about it later."
- "It is okay if my personal sleep requirements are different than someone else's."
- "The more I practice the techniques I have learned, the faster I will fall asleep. Sleeping pills are not a good long term solution anyway."
- "My insomnia plays less of a role in me getting sick than how I treat my body while I am awake."
- "I feel awful right now, but some of that is because I feel negatively because of my sleep. If I work to gain a positive mindset, I will be able to power through it all."
- "There is a solution that will work for me, and the work I am doing now with CBT-I will undoubtedly help at least a little."
- "I may not feel rested, but my brain and body did rest last night."
- "Insomnia is a very common illness, and there is nothing wrong with me for having it."

Schedule Worry Time

I know firsthand how tempting it can be to lay in bed and spend hours worrying over sleep, things that will happen tomorrow, and things that already have happened. As easy as it is to settle down and worry during bedtime, it is way more efficient and healthier for your insomnia for you to schedule time to worry. This allows you to vent your frustrations before bedtime so that you do not feel as if you have canned up all of your worries, and so that they do not interrupt your sleep time. One of my personal recommendations is to journal or write down things that you are worried about, because writing allows the brain to parse through anxiety more effectively.

The best way to schedule your worry time is devoting a specific time of day to your worries. This might be best scheduled at night after work, school, or any time way before bedtime. It is best not to start or end your day with negativity. Ensure that you have 10-30 minutes set aside, and focus on airing out your worries. These worries can pertain to any area of your life including sleep. It is important to do this even if you think it has nothing to do with your insomnia; the worries and anxieties you accumulate during the day can heighten in your mind subconsciously and create symptoms of insomnia. Setting aside time to worry frees space in your mind until the next session. Write things down that you're worried about, crumple up the paper, and throw it in the trash if you'd like. This sends the symbolic message to your mind that you have freed yourself from that worry, at least for now.

Scheduling worry time is a guaranteed way to reduce the amount of time you spend awake dwelling on something that happened in the past or something that will happen the next day.

My Story

I have personal experience with thoughts hindering my ability to sleep well, which is why I feel so confident speaking on the solutions to this problem. Earlier in my life, I had a tendency to stay up late finishing projects. I thought I could make up the sleep I missed on the weekends, or if I was really tired I'd just fall asleep. Now, I can recognize that these beliefs only served to worsen my insomnia. Night after night, I struggled to fall asleep, tossing and turning for hours on end. No matter what, I could not fall asleep and worried about the rest I was missing out on. This worry made it even more difficult to fall asleep. Cognitive restructuring was one of the key tools that saved me from this cycle.

This chapter undoubtedly revealed a troubling truth: you hold many unhealthy beliefs about sleep. You should now have a handful of tips in your toolbox to restructure these thoughts and form a more healthy outlook on sleep. In the next chapter, we're going to go over sleep hygiene that promotes healthy and restful sleep and allows you to be more awake and present during the day.

Chapter 7:
Clean Sweep for Clean Sleep

Did you know that new research has shown a link between sleep patterns and how someone perceives themselves aging (Sabatini et al., 2021)? According to research conducted by the University of Exeter, those with unhealthy sleeping habits tend to perceive themselves and their age more negatively. In fact, those studied reported both feeling older and feeling more negative about aging in general. The benefits of developing healthy sleep routines and mindsets now is invaluable. The effects of poor sleep affect you throughout your lifetime, especially as you age.

Another excellent way to improve the quality of your sleep and your ability to rest well is sleep hygiene. Sleep hygiene might sound like doing the laundry or cleaning the room, but that is not exactly what sleep hygiene is. It is definitely a good idea to have clean bedding and a clean room, but sleep hygiene is a bit more complex. Sleep hygiene is a combination of the environment and habits you engage with that result in consistent and healthy sleep patterns (Suni, 2020). This includes maintaining a sleep schedule, keeping the bedroom cozy, and having good sleep habits like a routine and set wake up and bedtimes. Good sleep hygiene is important because it is beneficial in more ways than one. Sleep hygiene can improve mental and physical health, and result in a better overall quality of life, which is nothing to sneeze at. Good habits are essential to maintaining a healthy lifestyle, and that goes for sleep too.

Assuming that at least some of your symptoms of insomnia stem from poor sleep hygiene, following a consistent set of sleep hygiene regulations should improve your sleep quality overall.

Sleep Hygiene Recommendations

Sleep hygiene is going to look a little different for each person, but there are some general guidelines you should follow regarding sleep hygiene. For example, if you need to eat or drink within an hour of going to sleep, you should only be eating a light snack and drinking water. As I mentioned earlier, no caffeine consumption within six hours of going to bed. Caffeine is a great way to ensure a disruption to sleep hygiene. Another important piece of nutritional advice is to avoid using alcohol as a means of putting yourself to sleep. Not only is alcohol bad for your overall health, but the ensuing addiction from becoming reliant on alcohol to sleep is going to hurt you drastically.

If your home is noisy, inside or out, a good part of sleep hygiene is making sure to control those noises. Sometimes we can not do anything about this, like when the interfering noise is traffic or construction. In this case, the best options are earplugs or white noise. White noise is also good for people who struggle to sleep in silence, because it is generally soothing and not disruptive. White noise is a good alternative to TV or music at night.

As much as this may pain you to hear, it is also a good idea to try sleeping without your pets in the bed. Pet fur and dander are allergens that can dirty your living space, especially your bed, and pets like cats and dogs notoriously run on different sleep schedules than human beings do. Even if you are not prone to animal related allergies, particles of dead skin, fur, dust, and germs too small to be noticed by the human eye are still incredibly harmful when inhaled, and can therefore contribute to respiratory problems that hinder sleep. If you absolutely are not willing to negotiate closing your pet out of the bedroom at night, I highly suggest at least getting them a separate bed to place on the floor, and allowing them a way out of the room at night. That way your beloved pet is still nearby and can exit the room without interrupting you. This does still run the risk of being woken up early by a hyperactive cat or dog, but it is a far better alternative to sleeping with your pet in the same bed.

Remember, two things you should always do are maintaining a regular sleep schedule and keeping a comfortable sleep environment. Not only are these things part of conditioning, restriction, and control for improving sleeping, but they are also emphasized in sleep hygiene techniques.

It is ideal to follow these rules to the best of your ability until you notice yourself sleeping well at night. At that point, you can consider very slowly implementing changes to your sleep hygiene, like letting your pet in the room or consuming alcohol on special occasions. Try to avoid making drastic changes, though, because this can ruin the progress you have made with your insomnia. Change one thing at a time, and if you notice the quality of your sleep start to decrease afterwards, either you have changed something vital or have not allowed your body and mind enough time to adjust to your routine.

Sleep hygiene is a vital part of getting a good night's sleep, but it is not the only factor. Relaxation techniques are also essential and can have a positive impact on your stress levels, thus providing you with the ability to rest more easily at night. Our next chapter is going to focus on how to develop these techniques and what techniques you can personally implement.

Product Suggestions

Sleeping should by no means be a costly endeavor. However, if you feel like splurging a bit on improving the quality of your sleep, or are looking for specific products to aid in your insomnia healing journey, there are a few highly rated products online that can be purchased to improve the quality of sleep or your sleep routine:

- Weighted blankets. Some people who experience anxiety tend to find solace in weighted blankets, which provide equal pressure across the entire body at night. I would suggest starting with a 10-pound or lighter weighted blanket, as they can get both pricy and heavier than you might think! Weighted blankets can be used on their own as well as underneath or on

top of your regular bedding, depending on what is most comfortable to you.
- A tasty drink you love for nighttime. Some good ideas are chamomile or other herbal, caffeine free teas and drinks that are easy on the stomach and promote relaxation. Drinks you enjoy can be part of your nightly routine, but be sure to avoid drinking lots of liquid right before bed–no one wants to wake up in the middle of the night just to use the restroom. Plus, doing so is counterintuitive for our mission here. Give yourself an hour or two for the drink to settle before bedtime.
- An eye mask and ear plugs, to keep out light and sound respectively. A lot of people benefit from complete silence and darkness while sleeping, but that is something that is not always possible in every neighborhood. Purchasing these items is relatively cheap and can up the quality of your sleep significantly.
- If you are someone who needs some low lighting to sleep, it is time to ditch the TV. A more natural, soothing alternative for lighting is a himalayan salt lamp, which are usually sold for cheap online or in stores. Remember, it is best to leave your lamp plugged in or in a dry space, because moisture and the cold can cause the salt crystals to dissolve (yes, it is real salt!).
- Silk pillowcases and high thread count sheets are wonderful for your hair and skin. These can run you a bit of money depending on how much you care for quality, especially if you take them to be cleaned professionally, but many people find these items well worth the cost.
- Lightly scented bedding items, stuffed animals, oils, etc. Scents like lavender, vanilla, and chamomile are lovely and soothing, and scented sleep products are often cheap. They come in various shapes and sizes for all types of sleepers. You can also purchase a lightly scented candle for the nightstand, but if you light it, be sure to never sleep with the candle burning.
- White noise machines as well as brown noise devices are fantastic for background noise for those of us who need a little background sound for a restful sleep. You can also utilize Alexa or your devices you already own to play white or brown noise.

- Humidifiers or diffusers are good options both for scent and preventing the room from being too dry.

I am not endorsed by nor do I sell any of the above products. If you are looking for ways to improve the bedroom or your nightly routine and have the extra time, money, or desire, picking out a few products to improve your sleep is well worth it. Most of the products above are relatively cheap or have cheap alternatives as well, so there is no need to break the bank for sleep!

Low-Income Sleep Hygiene

My goal is to help as many people as possible heal from the symptoms of insomnia. A lot of these tips may seem inaccessible to people who are enduring poverty or struggles related to low income. Because I want to make sure everyone is heard and helped, I think it is necessary to touch on what you can do if you are someone who is low-income and are unable to afford central air, sleep products, etc.

One of the best things you can do that is cost efficient for low-income households is to invest in a box fan or window air conditioning unit, both of which are far cheaper options compared to paying for central heating and air. This way you are still able to help create an environment cool enough for you to sleep in. Fans that plug into the wall can also be a good way to create non-distracting background noise if a white noise machine is not in your budget. When using one of these fans, it is best to not have the fan aimed directly at you. If you can, try to point the fan so that it blows air into the center of the room. Or, if the fan can oscillate, use that setting. It will make the room far more comfortable to sleep in without running the risk of you becoming too cold in the middle of the night.

Sleep masks and ear plugs are often sold at the dollar store for one to five dollars, and can definitely be a lifesaver if you live near traffic or construction. It is also possible to still create a comfortable bed on a low income. For uncomfortable mattresses, mattress toppers are often a much cheaper alternative to make a bed feel soft and plush. From my experience, even the cheapest ones available do wonders and are worth spending money on. Also, a cozy comforter or a handful of soft blankets can be just as if not more comfortable than expensive bedding. It is still possible to sleep well as someone on a low income; you just have to know how to adapt certain things to suit your needs.

Chapter 8:
Kick Back and Relax

"Learn to relax. Your body is precious, as it houses your mind and spirit. Inner peace begins with a relaxed body." – Norman Vincent Peale

Relaxation techniques are another way to improve the quality of your sleep. The things you do throughout the day and just before bed all play some role in impacting the quality of your rest at night.

Relaxation techniques work more than just mentally; they are scientifically effective as well. Throughout the day, your mind and body faces stress, even if you do not realize it. Anything from nearly dropping something to worrying that you will be late can cause stress on your mind and body, and without relaxation techniques you allow that stress to continuously build up. Relaxation techniques work on a scientific level by lowering blood pressure, improving mood and digestion, and alleviating muscle tension and pain (Breus, 2022).

Relaxation Techniques

There are hundreds if not thousands of options available for relaxation techniques, so it is absolute that one will work for you.

One valuable relaxation technique involves diaphragm breathing. Your diaphragm is a muscle in your stomach that helps you breathe, the same one that is responsible for the uncomfortable sensation of hiccups. If you have ever participated in choir or band, your instructor likely already explained to you what your diaphragm is in depth. If you do not know, your diaphragm is located near your sternum. If you breathe in deeply, you may be able to feel your diaphragm–it's in that spot that gets tight in your lower chest as your lungs fill with air.

Diaphragm breathing engages this muscle, and has many benefits. Diaphragm breathing has been known to lower stress and blood pressure levels, and is great for many other health benefits too (Jewell & Hoshaw, 2021).

In order to practice diaphragm breathing, you first need to be sitting or lying on a comfortable, flat surface. The position you are in depends on what is most comfortable for you, but I recommend sitting up for now. Make sure you are not holding any tension in your shoulders; allow them to drop fully instead of being forced up near your ears. Then, put one hand on your stomach and the other on your chest. Do not strain to do so, but once your hands are in position, breathe in through your nose as much as you can. Feel the air flow through your nose and into your belly, and let your hand notice it expand. Then, form an "o" shape with your lips and gently exhale, noticing your stomach shrinking again. Do this at least five times for the best results, and you should feel much calmer afterwards. This is a breathing exercise commonly used in meditation and anxiety relieving CBT practices, and it can help you find a moment of calm if you are particularly tense.

Another breathing exercise you can try is called the 4-7-8 technique. A lot of mental health professionals encourage people to utilize this technique because it has many benefits. The 4-7-8 technique is good for providing sufficient oxygen to your organs and blood, and this technique is also very good for the nervous system (Gotter, 2018). Some individuals even report success curing symptoms of insomnia solely by dedicating time to practice this technique.

In order to perform the 4-7-8 breathing technique, find a comfortable spot to sit or lay and ensure you are positioned with good posture. If you are trying to calm down, you can sit or lay, but if you want to do this specifically to try and fall asleep, you should do so lying down. Let the tip of your tongue rest on the top of your mouth behind the teeth, and do not move it for the duration of this process.

Exhale completely, then inhale from your nose while you count to four silently. Hold your breath for a seven count, then exhale for eight seconds. Continue doing this for at least four cycles to benefit from the practice. After doing so, you should feel much calmer.

Guided imagery is another fantastic relaxation technique you can practice in order to sleep better at night. Guided imagery is a type of meditation you may be familiar with if you practice guided meditation often. This practice involves concentrating on something specific, most often a natural scene or event, in order to calm down. This is a relaxation technique that is good for lowering stress and muscle tension and slowing the mind down (Nunez, 2020). Practicing this technique is known to reduce anxiety and pain as well as to improve sleep. All you need to try guided imagery meditation is a comfortable, quiet spot. Some people like guided audio for their meditation practices, which can be found easily on YouTube.

Follow these steps to guide you through your first guided imagery practice:

1. Sit or lie down comfortably somewhere that you will not be interrupted for at least 15 minutes.
2. Close your eyes, and start to breathe deeply. You will want to continue deep breathing until the meditation is over.
3. Imagine your guided imagery scene. If you do not know where to start, I am going to provide you with a guided imagery script after these instructions.
4. Stay relaxed and imagine your scene for at least 15 minutes. You can, of course, relax longer if you would like.
5. After your time is up, slowly bring your mind out of the scene by focusing on your breath. After three breath cycles, open your eyes.

Guided imagery works best in combination with other practices. You can combine the above methods of breathing relaxation into your guided meditation, or you can practice meditating after something like progressive muscle relaxation, which I will talk about shortly.

As I mentioned, if you are not sure what scene to start with, here is a guided imagery script I wrote for myself that you can use in your personal practices. Feel free to alter any scenes or details to your liking to provide optimal relaxation.

"Find a relaxing spot, and get into the position you will hold for this meditation. Close your eyes softly, or hold a gentle gaze if that is more comfortable. Starting with your head, notice each part of your body slowly relaxing. Release all tension from your mouth, eyes, neck, shoulders, chest, arms and legs, etc., until your entire body is free from tension. Breathe in, and notice how the breath travels down into your belly. Breathe out, and breathe in again, feeling the air spread to your body, sharing its gift of life with each extremity. Let it reach your fingertips, soothe, and soak in. Exhale. Continue breathing with awareness until your body finds its natural, relaxed pace to breathe at.

"Your body should be fully relaxed. Imagine yourself in a warm, light coat, standing on a path in a forest. Notice the color of the leaves on the trees; maybe it has just turned fall and the leaves are a brilliant amber, or maybe spring is around the corner and the trees are sprouting leaves for the summer. Notice what you can hear. Maybe it is the wind, the bristle of leaves. Walk slowly along the path, enjoying your journey. Notice the rocks you come across, unique patterns in the trees you pass.

"As you continue to walk, you come into a clearing with a small river to the side. The grass is tall and overgrown, but natural. There is so much peace enveloping you, and you walk to the side of the river. Sit down next to the river, and notice your reflection in the clear waters. Is there anything swimming? How fast is the pond moving? Maybe you let your fingertips skim the surface of the water; how does it feel? Find appreciation in your heart for the ability to share this moment with the nature around you, and continue on the path.

"As you walk, the path curves and you come to a small cottage. It is a deep brown, and you notice all of the little details of how the cottage is built. All of its unique markings and patterns. It looks so comfortable and safe. That cottage is yours, you realize, so you go inside. Notice how the wood sounds as you walk up the steps from the stone path and across the porch. Notice the way the door knob feels in your hand as you turn it.

"Make your way inside, slipping out of your coat and draping it over a chair nearby. You sit down and think about all of the beauty you saw on your walk, knowing you can go back on that walk any time the stress of life overwhelms you. It lies just at your doorstep.

"Slowly, allow your focus to come back to your breathing. Hold onto the feelings of calm and peace as you return to awareness and finish off your meditation."

If you like that script for meditating, you can use it as much as you need to; the fun part of guided imagery is that it can follow you anywhere you go. Guided imagery is an incredibly useful method of relaxation that I personally love.

The final method of relaxation I am going to tell you about is progressive muscle relaxation, or PMR, which I mentioned earlier. PMR was developed in the 1920s by Edmund Jacobson with the idea that physically relaxing the body can cause mental relaxation as well (Nunez, 2020). PMR takes advantage of the fact that by tensing a muscle and then releasing it, your muscles become more relaxed. This is done by focusing on each area of the body one at a time, and relies on tensing the muscles further before relaxing them in order to feel more benefits from the technique.

PMR is a useful relaxation technique because it reduces anxiety and pain, improves sleep, and brings the blood pressure to a healthy level. Those who suffer from migraines also find that PMR decreases the frequency of migraine episodes. In order to perform PMR, follow these steps:

1. Sit or lay down and relax the body. Begin breathing slowly and deeply until your breathing finds a consistent, calm rhythm.
2. Start with the feet. Raise your toes up as tensely as you can, and hold them that way for a few seconds. Release the hold, then do the same thing again but by flexing your toes downward.
3. Tense your calves as tight as you can and release.
4. Press your knees together as tight as you can, then release.
5. Tighten your thigh muscles and release.
6. Clench your hands into fists as tight as possible and let go.
7. Repeat the same actions with your arms, glutes, stomach, and chest.
8. Raise your shoulders up to your ears and then release them.
9. Tense your lips and release, then open your mouth wide and release.

10. Close your eyes tightly, release, and open them as wide as you can. Release again.

Ideally, this should take about 15 minutes, and you should maintain the same deep, calm breaths throughout the practice.

Journaling for Sleep

Journaling is a fantastic way to relax the mind; writing things down allows us to unload doubts, worries, and more. Positive journaling reminds us why we love being alive, and journaling to vent is great on the brain. If you do not currently have a stable journaling routine, it is something that I would definitely recommend. Developing a journaling habit can be a bit challenging at first, but with dedication it is something that can prove itself to be incredibly rewarding.

For those who do not know where to start, just grab a pen and a notebook! A lot of people journal on their phone, but it is well known that the effects of journaling are best observed when you handwrite what is on your mind instead. I encourage you to practice journaling by hand. Once you have a journal to work with, either set a timer for ten minutes or make it a goal to write for an entire page. Write for that duration, and then you can either stop, finish your thought, or journal until you feel done—just do not get so caught up in journaling that it distracts you from your rest. You should do this every day, preferably around the same time of day, to establish a journaling habit.

Whether you want to journal in the morning, at night, or to relax yourself when frustrated, here are some good journal prompts you can use to soothe your mind, and either unload a negative day or remind yourself of the positives in your life:

- Something that is worrying me the most right now is…
- Today, I am grateful for…
- I am looking forward to…
- Something I regret doing today is…
- Today, I learned that…

- My current bedtime routine looks like... I can improve this in a way that optimizes my sleep by...
- My current morning routine looks like... I can create a better start to my day by...
- Today, I cared for myself by...
- Right now, I think the state of my mental health is... because... I can improve upon this by...
- Last night, I dreamed about...
- When I am really worried about something, some things I can do to soothe myself include...
- Something that made me feel bad today was... To keep this from happening again, I will...
- I am proud of myself because...
- A habit I need to break is...
- My favorite memory is...
- One of my biggest goals in life right now is...
- Tomorrow, I will be a better person by...
- I feel most like myself when...
- Something I would tell my 10-year-old self is...
- A new habit I want to develop is...
- The things I value most in life are...
- I am grateful for the people in my life, specifically... I can show them my gratitude by...
- On nights I struggle with falling asleep, something I notice is that...
- On my best nights, something I notice is that...
- One place I have visited that made me feel safe was...

You do not have to take any of those and run with them; in fact, I encourage you to create your own prompts or use ones that you like more if you have an idea of something that might resonate more. Otherwise, you can follow the prompts I have given you, or write whatever comes to your mind. Journaling will help your mind be at ease and will give you a physical outlet for anything on your mind, clearing up tension and stress and allowing you to have a much better night's rest.

On the Go

We have already discussed the effect that stress has on being unable to sleep or exacerbating insomnia symptoms. For many of us, though, we face stress while we're out and about at work, the grocery store, or somewhere else where we feel so overwhelmingly tense that we need to find a moment of calm right then. Being able to calm yourself down from a tense moment is a good way to reduce your stress overall in order to prevent stress from interfering with your sleep.

There are many techniques you can use to soothe yourself during a busy, stressful day. Breathing exercises mentioned above are all possible to use, but what if that is not enough at work or the store? I've got you covered.

One method for calming yourself down is by grounding. Grounding is a technique recommended by most, if not all, mental health professionals. It involves centralizing your energy and thoughts in order to reconnect yourself with the world around you. There are a lot of different explanations as to how grounding works, both scientific and spiritual. Scientifically, it works the same as meditation does, soothing stress, improving mental well-being, and even having such impacts as lowering pain and improving sleep. On a spiritual level, grounding involves a metaphysical sort of reconnection with the energies flowing through the earth, which helps to take you out of your brain and remove you from your worries. Regardless of whichever explanation aligns with you the most, grounding is a wonderful way to calm yourself down on the go.

There are lots of grounding techniques available. One that is highly recommended for those with anxiety is called the 5-4-3-2-1 technique. If you notice that a lot of things mentioned in this chapter follow numerical naming, that is for a reason! Following patterns based on rhythms or counting is a very simple way to calm the mind and body. The 5-4-3-2-1 technique is simple and is meant to bring your attention back to your surroundings instead of being held by your inner thoughts. You do not even need to be sitting or holding anything to do this, because the only tool involved is your senses. What you are going to do is try to steady your breathing as mentioned for other relaxation techniques. It is important to find a nice, slow rhythm that is comfortable. Then, you are going to name the following:

- 5 things you see
- 4 things you can touch
- 3 things you can hear
- 2 things you can smell
- 1 thing you can taste

You can also use your senses in other ways to ground yourself. A method I really like is using water, like in a sink in a public restroom. What you are going to do for this method is to just run your hands under the water. You should use either hot or cold water, not room temperature, but the water should not be uncomfortably hot or cold either. Let the water run over your hands and think about how it feels: does the water feel the same on all parts of your hand? How does it feel running between your fingers? How does the water make you feel? Once you are ready, switch the water to the other temperature and do the same thing. This helps you connect to the physical feeling of the water instead of the feelings inside of your mind.

You can also ground on the go by carrying something lightly scented to focus on. Essential oils work great for this, but be careful not to inhale or apply undiluted essential oils to the skin. If you have a good memory and like poetry, quotes, the Bible, or anything else you find worth memorizing, memorizing passages to recite to yourself is a good way to ground as well.

Employing any one or a combination of these grounding techniques is a wonderful way to manage stress throughout the day to ensure that it does not disturb your ability to rest well at night.

Relaxing Morning Routines

Deciding what to include in your morning routine can be a bit daunting; there are so many options for what to do to help wake yourself up and start your day. Because everyone's lifestyle is a bit different, I've decided to include a few different sample morning routines that you can either use directly or adapt to your needs, or just use as inspiration to create your own entirely unique routine. Whichever way you go, this will help you see what a healthy morning routine should look like.

One example of a healthy morning routine could go something like this:
1. Wake up, and before getting out of bed, do some simple stretches. Stretch out your arms, shoulders, spine, and legs, as you wake up and get ready to get out of bed.
2. If you feel tempted to go on your phone, avoid doing so. Instead, opt for reading a few lines from your favorite book or journaling.
3. Get up, open the curtains to let the sun in, and drink a glass of water. Now is a good time to make your bed. Remember, if the bed is made, you will be less likely to climb back in. Plus, you will get a good start to your nighttime routine with a fresh, organized room.
4. Brush your teeth, wash your face, and shower if you shower in the morning. If you would like, take some time now to say some positive affirmations while looking in the mirror, or set a goal or tone for the day.
5. Make yourself a nutritious, balanced breakfast and enjoy it by an open window or on the porch, getting in some good vitamin D for the day. You should also drink another glass of water, either by itself or alongside your morning drink of choice.
6. At this point, you can check your phone and get on with the rest of your day.

A good morning routine for early risers (people who get up before the sun) who need to be out the door could go something like this:
1. One of the best things you can do to plan for a morning routine where you have to leave the house relatively early is to prepare the night before. This means filling water bottles, making food and/or breakfast, setting up the coffee maker so that it is ready to go at the push of a button, laying out clothes to wear, etc.

2. Wake up and avoid hitting the snooze button. Leave your phone on the nightstand and give yourself some time to stretch. Drink some water too. Then, make your bed so that it is ready for tonight.
3. Go to start your coffee maker. If you exercise, now is a good time to fit that in; your coffee will be done and hot when you are done, and you will be able to shower after exercising so you are fresh and clean.
4. Drink your coffee, shower, and dress. Take some time to say a few positive affirmations or set a good goal for yourself in order to start your day off with a kick of positivity and motivation.
5. Make sure you eat a balanced breakfast and ensure that you have enough food and snacks—ones full of nutrition—for the day ahead.
6. Before you leave the house, do something that is good for your mind. Be it journaling, reading, a craft, spending time with pets, etc., make sure you do something to make you happy before starting the day.

For parents, depending on the age of your kids and if you have to get them ready for school or daycare, the morning can be an especially hectic time of day. Because of this, it is often hard for parents, especially those raising a child alone, to find a morning routine that works for them. This is something I experienced personally as well. Instead of trying to follow through with a streamlined routine, determine what works best for you. Some things you can consider include:

- When can I fit some me time into the morning schedule?
- Is my child more calm or more rowdy? Children who are more calm are far easier to incorporate into activities like your own breakfast eating, getting ready, etc.
- Is my child old enough to have their own morning routine? If your child is old enough to speak sentences and feed themselves, chances are they're old enough to follow some steps of a morning routine. This sets your child up to succeed in having a healthy relationship with their sleep routines as well. Encouraging your child to brush their own teeth and hair, dress

themselves, get out supplies for breakfast, pack their bag for school, etc. are all good things to include in a morning routine for a child. Positive reinforcement will go a long way in aiding your child to habitually follow their own routine.

Something else that might need to be accounted for is people who work night shifts and therefore have to wake up much later in the day, because they clock out late at night or early in the morning. In order to still achieve a good wakeup routine, some tips you can utilize are

Following a good sleep routine before bed.
Still getting some sunlight before you head off to work. Afternoon sun is just as helpful as morning sun, and seeing the daylight first thing will help your brain wake up as well as allow for you to absorb some of the vitamin D you miss out on by being a night owl.
Your sleep and wake times should still be consistent, even if they are not what most people consider to be appropriate. Getting your body used to one sleep schedule will maximize your sleep.

Remember, you can personalize your morning routine to fit your needs. What works for my morning and my life will not necessarily fit perfectly into yours, and that is alright. What is important is that you wake up gently, drink some water, get some sunlight, and avoid going on your phone for at least a half hour after you wake up in order to allow your brain time to adjust without the interference of electronics. This goes for televisions too. For morning entertainment, try something like music, crossword puzzles, or reading.

Also, it is possible that you do not sleep in your bed alone because you have a partner or spouse that you sleep with. It is perfect if you two can maintain the same sleep schedule, but oftentimes one person has to be up before the other person for work, school, or childcare. You can still have a good morning despite this. Talk to your partner about what you both can do to respect each other's time in the morning, and see what needs to be adjusted. If you wake up earlier, be prepared to be more careful with your wake up routine to not disturb your partner; if your partner wakes up earlier, ensure that you are not interrupting their sleep and vice versa. For alarm clocks and lights, a good set of ear plugs and an eye mask will help make conflicting morning routines work more smoothly.

Relaxing Bedtime Routines

Now that we've covered potential routines you can follow for your morning routine as well as considerations, tips, and tricks depending on various facets of different lifestyles, I want to talk a bit about specific examples for healthy bedtime routines. Forming a bedtime routine, in my opinion, is far easier than forming a morning routine. It is much harder to get out of bed than it is to get into bed for most people. Nevertheless, I do want to show you potential routines that you can take or adapt to your needs.

One example of a healthy routine for someone going to bed could go like this:

1. About an hour and a half before bed, begin the process of winding down. Set any alarms you need for the night, finish texting whoever you need to, turn your phone on do not disturb and leave it on the charger for the night.
2. If you like to drink tea or other (non-alcoholic and non-caffeinated) beverages to relax yourself, get that done first. That way, your body can digest the drink and you will not be interrupted in the middle of the night.
3. Do some light stretches–nothing that will hurt or raise your heartrate.
4. If you shower before bed, now's a good time to do that. Get dressed in your sleep clothes (it is good to have designated pajamas to let your brain know that it is time for rest), and sit down somewhere.
5. Make sure you are relaxing in dim lighting, and do one of the relaxation techniques I suggested in a previous chapter to soothe your mind and prepare it for rest.
6. Now is also a wonderful time to journal about your day.
7. With whatever time you have left before bedtime, do something you enjoy that will not hinder your rest. Remember,

no screen time! Reading a book, doing a craft, or something else that allows you to just relax.
8. As it gets closer to bedtime, get ready to say your prayers or any final things you need to do just before sleep. Turn on your white noise, turn off your lights, and climb in bed.
9. Close your eyes and enjoy a peaceful night's sleep!

If that sounds rather empty for a night time routine, even boring for some people, that is on purpose; your sleep routine should focus on calming the mind down and relaxing, not on stimulation. Doing things that excite the mind just before bed will prevent you from a restful sleep, because your brain will still be in high gear once your head hits the pillow. Nighttime routines are easier to form because not only do they require less steps, but they are incredibly easy to move to any bedtime you need. Whether you go to bed at 7 p.m. or 12 a.m., two people can share the same night time routine if that works for them.

In case you are not sure what activities you might want to do that are restful before bed, here is a list of some activities that I personally love doing to wind down in the evening:

Puzzles
Adult coloring pages
Reading (paperback books, especially the Bible)
Prayer
Meditation
Making friendship bracelets or other small crafts
This can include knitting, crochet, and embroidery
Journaling

For parents, it is a good idea to try to fit in at least a few minutes of personal time before you go to sleep, even if you have to physically put a young child to bed. As with morning routines, consider whether your child is able to join you in your routine peacefully, would benefit from their own, or if they're entirely independent enough to make their own choices about bedtime rituals on their own. Many parents, especially nowadays, are opting to co-sleep with their young ones, which is something I've enjoyed myself. A good way to wind down for co-sleepers is to find a relaxing activity that you and your child can do together. For instance, both of you could color together to wind down, your child with a kid's coloring book and you with an adult one. That way, your bedtime rituals serve not just as a method of relaxation, but as a bonding experience too. Providing your child with the tools they need to have a healthy relationship with bedtime and sleep is instrumental in preventing insomnia from developing later on for them.

And for those of you who work on irregular schedules, fret not! You can still have a soothing bedtime routine even if your bedtime is in the morning. I would recommend blackout curtains for your home, and to close them before you leave for work. When you come home, you will be able to enter a dimmer environment as opposed to a bright one more useful for a morning routine, and you will be able to settle into a routine far easier. This will also allow you to be able to let more light in once you wake up, stimulating your brain with the light. Remember, around an hour and a half before you need to be asleep is a good time to stop any disruptive activities like screen usage.

Night time routines are something I personally adore, because it is time dedicated to myself and relaxation. Your bedtime routine should be something you enjoy that calms your mind, and be something that you can look forward to as a part of your day. A strong bedtime routine is an amazing step forward in fighting insomnia and developing a healthy mindset towards rest.

Try This Out!

Various apps are on the market to help with relaxation, most of them focusing on meditation and deep breathing. They do an excellent job at combining the above relaxation methods to provide you with the optimal experience, all from the comfort of your cell phone. Download one or more of the following apps and see which one you prefer:

- Calm
- Headspace
- Aura
- Simple Habit

- Smiling Mind

Most of the above apps focus on allowing you to relax and guided meditations.

Relaxation techniques can be a powerful tool for improving our sleep due to all of the benefits they provide. There is definitely more you can do to improve your sleep, and that includes focusing on proper nutrition. Eating well can play a vital role in getting the rest we need; healthy, nutrient-rich foods are necessary to sleep well and maintain health.

Chapter 9:
Good Food, Good Night

*"One cannot think well, love well, sleep well, if one has not dined well." –
Virginia Woolf, A Room of One's Own*

Diet and Nutrition

Nutrition is one of the many key factors that can prohibit you from getting a restful night's sleep. Working to improve your nutritional health can do worlds of wonder for relieving you of insomnia. Even if you think you eat fairly healthy now, you will probably soon realize that some of your eating habits and nutritional beliefs can be contributing to worse overall health that also plays a role in insomnia.

If someone says to you that it is important to have good nutrition, it is entirely possible that you might not know what that even means. Nutritional education, especially in the US, is incredibly lacking nowadays, but do not worry! I've got all the tips you will need for improving your nutrition in order to quell your insomnia.

Nutrition is the way that you power your body via food. Each day, bustling around, working, talking, and even resting deplete the nutrients from the day before, so it is necessary to replace those nutrients each day. This includes drinking water and eating a balanced meal thrice a day, as well as ensuring your diet is rich in vitamins. You cannot say you have a healthy diet if you do not consume lots of fresh fruit and vegetables every day. The more vibrant in color the better. Your diet should also contain protein, whole grains, and dairy. Good nutrition is not just about what you should be eating; it is also about what food you should avoid. Excess salt, oil, sugar, and fats can be bad for your overall health and cause complications with your heart or lead to diabetes. For those deficient in key vitamins, consulting a doctor and discussing supplement options is the best course of action.

So why does this matter to your insomnia? The types of food you eat impact your metabolism, bodily function, and energy levels. If your body does not have the food it needs to survive, it starts stripping those nutrients from the brain. Maintaining good nutrition will provide you with enough energy for your brain to know when to wake and when to sleep, among other things.

It can be hard to start eating a balanced diet if you are not familiar with nutritional or food science. In the most basic sense, a balanced diet is a diet that gives your body the right vitamins and nutrients it needs to function daily. You should eat a combination of vitamins, carbs, healthy fat, and protein by eating dairy, fruits and veggies, protein from lean meat or beans, tofu, and legumes, and whole grains. You should avoid processed food like chips and lunch meats, sugar and salt in excess, red meat, and alcohol as much as possible.

Also remember that not every body is the same and therefore needs different things to be healthy. The best way to eat a healthy meal is to have half of your meal be fruits and vegetables, half being grains and proteins, and a side of dairy being added. What you do not eat in one meal should be made up for in another. If you have concerns about your nutritional health, discussing nutrition plans with a doctor or dietitian will ensure that you are eating what is best for you specifically.

Many people who struggle with nutritional health rely on supplements like vitamins to make up for that. It is perfectly alright to take dietary supplements if you truly are unable to keep your body healthy solely off of food, but this is a decision to discuss with the appropriate professionals. Too much of a good thing turns into a bad thing quickly, and that goes for supplements too. Generally speaking, supplements are most appropriate for those with food allergies, people who are pregnant, people who are unable to eat certain foods for some reason, and similar situations. If you eat a lot of different kinds of healthy foods, you likely do not need supplements.

With regard to sleep specifically, there are three essential vitamins to improve the quality of your rest. Those are B-complex vitamins, magnesium, and vitamin D. B-complex vitamins are incredibly important to your body's ability to produce melatonin. You have likely heard of B vitamins before; they include vitamins like B12 and B6, vitamins food products like to advertise they contain. For good reason too, because the best way to get B vitamins is through natural sources of food. If you are lacking in B vitamins, you can usually find them in eggs and dairy as well as anything high in protein. Magnesium is a vitamin many people take in the form of supplements because it can often be hard to get from food for many people. The addition of magnesium in your diet is known to relieve insomnia and improve the quality of sleep among people who experience these things. For foods, you can gain magnesium from nuts and seeds as well as bananas. And finally, vitamin D. You probably know that vitamin D is the vitamin we get from the sun, but what a lot of people do not know is that simply taking a vitamin D supplement does not do all of the work. Even if you take a supplement, you still need to go outside. This goes hand in hand with ensuring that you get sunlight during the daytime as a method of relieving insomnia. Vitamin D can also be garnered from things like milk.

The Link Between Sleep and Nutrition

The state of your nutritional health is connected deeply to your ability to sleep and your ability to sleep well at that. Your nutritional health connects directly to how restorative your sleep at night is, so it is important to maintain a strong relationship with nutritional health.

For example, if you do not get enough fiber or the right fats in your diet, you can become a very light sleeper who wakes up sporadically. Sugary food and drinks can lead to trouble falling asleep or staying asleep. Furthermore, eating or drinking heavy or caffeinated foods can disrupt circadian rhythm cycles, causing you to be unable to fall asleep or stay asleep. This is because your body takes time to digest food, and by feeding your body late into the night, it sends signals to our brain that it is still time to be eating. This means your body is working too hard when it should be focused on being calm and relaxing (ENERGY BOOST COLUMN, 2020).

The food you eat can have many other impacts on your sleep too. For example, if you are postmenopausal and eat a diet consisting of a high glycemic index, you could suffer from worsened insomnia as a result of that diet (Gangwisch et al., 2019). Certain foods can also impact hormones that regulate your ability to sleep, such as foods with tryptophan. These foods can increase your brain's ability to produce melatonin (Tinsley, 2018). On the other hand, anything containing caffeine can lower melatonin production.

Foods to Avoid Before Bed

The following is a list of foods you should avoid going to bed. This list will help you determine which foods to avoid, but is not comprehensive.

Spicy or acidic foods, which can cause heartburn and disrupt your sleep. These foods can also raise your body temperature, and this is the exact opposite thing you want for bedtime.
Foods with caffeine. Check the nutrition labels of anything you eat before bed—you might be surprised as to which foods hide caffeine in their ingredients.
Sugary foods.
Alcohol.
Heavy foods, such as fatty or fried foods. These are hard to digest and can disrupt sleep.

Foods that Help You Sleep

Conversely, there are also a variety of foods that aid in your ability to sleep. Typically, these foods will have magnesium or nutrients that regulate melatonin and serotonin levels in the brain.

The following foods are good choices for improving your sleep:

- Nuts, which are high in magnesium.

- Kiwi. These contain many vitamins and have been linked to better sleep.
- Fatty fish, which is rife with vitamin D and omega-3s that help sleep.
- Cherries, especially tart ones, which can increase sleep times due to their melatonin levels.

- These foods are best consumed as snacks 2-3 hours before bedtime for the best effect. This gives the body enough time to digest them and allows their benefits to linger for the sleep process.

- **More Nutrition Tips**

- Understandably so, just listing off things you should and should not do is not enough to actually explain sleep related nutrients. Therefore, I am going to go a bit more in depth with some of the ideas above in order to explain some concepts a bit further.
- First, why is it bad to eat some foods before bedtime? It depends on the food specifically, but most of the foods above are bad to eat for sleep for two reasons: either they are a stimulant, or they have a tendency to cause inflammation. As far as stimulants go, it should be obvious why those are a bad choice for before bedtime—they stimulate the brain and the body. Caffeine, for example, gives the body more energy than it began with, which is not what you want before bed. Even if you believe that caffeine does not impact your ability to rest and that if you are tired you will sleep anyway, as I believed for years, that is not the case. Just because caffeine is not making you feel alert does not mean that it is not impacting your brain and heart. It is also vital to remember that many foods like chocolate contain caffeine in them that you would not expect, so it is important to read the nutritional labels of anything you plan to eat before bed. After you have familiarized yourself with certain foods, you can make a list of nighttime snacks that

are good for you and free of caffeine or inflammatory agents. It is a good idea to keep this list pinned to the fridge to serve as a reminder, especially if you are prone to go hunting for a midnight snack. Picking a food off of the list of approved snacks will do you far better.

- As far as inflammatory foods go, it is a little less clear why they are not good for before bedtime. Spicy or acidic foods are just a few of the Inflammatory foods. Inflammatory foods can cause stress or immune responses in the body, and it is similar to going to bed before food is undigested. Your body is unable to relax properly if it is full of inflammation due to spicy foods, so it is better to abstain from spicy foods until the next day. Other inflammatory foods include red meat, fried food, processed foods, and soda. Personally, I believe your best bet is to eat fresh berries and nuts as a snack if you are hungry around bedtime. The antioxidants in blueberries, for example, are stellar for the skin and nails, and nuts are high in vitamins that the body needs to sleep. Plus nuts can be incredibly filling if you find the right ones for yourself.

Another issue I'd like to address is regarding people who are in seemingly perfect nutritional health yet still have issues sleeping. I recently had an experience where I discovered that I have a variety of food allergies that manifest more like sensitivity. I do not have food allergies that will cause a severe reaction, but I am sensitive to lots of foods. This may be the case for you as well, even if you do not think you experience food sensitivity. Because it can be rather expensive to get checked for food sensitivities, my recommendation is to experiment a bit. If you notice you sleep poorly after eating certain foods throughout the day, try eliminating those foods from your diet and see what happens.

It is also possible that you are deficient in vitamins without knowing it. The most common vitamins that people are deficient in include vitamins C and D as well as magnesium. Eating foods that are rich in these vitamins as well as spending time in the sun is a good way to raise your vitamin levels and improve any potential deficiencies. Taking multivitamins is also a good idea, but I do recommend consulting with a doctor as to if this is in your best interest.

Another set of tips I have is specifically regarding cravings. Sometimes, even at night, you will crave a food that you are better off without at that time. What is fortunate is that usually when your body is craving something, it is because your body wants something else. Craving a food item is just your body's way of telling you that you are lacking a nutrient or vitamin that your body needs to function. It is especially helpful to know this if you often find yourself staying up at night because of an unwavering food craving. I've created a list of food items for you to reference below, which includes some of the most common cravings as well as what you can eat instead that the body will appreciate more and will not be unable to sleep because of. I will also explain what specifically your body needs that is causing that craving.

Cravings and their alternatives:

- If you are craving chocolate, it is because your body is craving magnesium. Instead of chocolate, some good sleep-friendly alternatives you can enjoy are nuts, beans, legumes, leafy greens, etc.
- If you find yourself craving sweet foods in general, your body is actually craving something called phosphorus, which is found in the bones in your body and is one of the most abundant minerals in the body. Instead of seeking sweet food, try to go for chicken, eggs, and nuts. Remember to avoid processed foods as you do so—fresh meats are always better for the body!
- For bread or pasta cravings, your body is not looking for bread or pasta specifically. What it is actually looking for is nitrogen, which takes care of the proteins and hormones in your body, and can be found in dark greens, nuts, and seeds. If you have not noticed by now, seeds and nuts are a fantastic catch all snack for those with cravings or bedtime hunger because they take care of so many different issues in the body.
- This can also be due to a lack of chromium in the body, which you can resolve by eating avocados.
- If you feel like you are unable to make it through the night without oily or fatty food, your body is actually sending the signal to you that you need calcium, which helps your bones

stay strong. Instead of oily foods that will sit in your stomach and digest slowly, preventing a good night's sleep, you can opt for several other foods. Any green vegetables as well as fruits like dates and plums should work well to quell your cravings.
- Soda cravings are also a sign that your body needs more calcium, so for a soda craving you can eat the same foods as you would in place of oily or fatty food.
- If you are experiencing cravings related to your menstrual cycle, what your body is actually in need of is zinc. Zinc can be found in leafy vegetables, root vegetables, and pumpkin seeds, just for a few examples.
- Salty food cravings can often be a sign that you need more salt, but because salt can cause bloating and inflammation, it is a good idea to try something else first. Salt cravings can also be a sign that you need more chloride and silicon, which you can get from nuts and seeds, celery, tomatoes, and lettuce.

Using the above ideas to quell hunger cravings instead of eating the food you actually think you want is going to be healthier for you in the long run, and result in much better sleep too.

Sleep-Friendly Exercise

For people who lead more active lifestyles or feel themselves brimming with excess energy despite insomnia, it can be hard to wind down at night. Even if you are tired, sometimes the body can feel jittery and in need of movement. Unfortunately, extreme or extensive exercise is counterproductive to a good night's sleep, because getting the heart rate up and moving around so much wakes the body up instead of working to sedate it. That does not mean that a little movement before bed is a lost cause, though. There are plenty of exercises you can do before bed that will help relax you and your mind without elevating your heart rate or stress levels.

A simple walk can be really great for getting out excess energy in the body, especially if you live in a particularly nice area. Heading outside to walk for 15-20 minutes before you start your bedtime routine is a remarkable way to burn off some excess energy. Plus, you will get to see the low lighting of the sun and breathe in some fresh air, which never hurts to relax the body a bit.

You also have a variety of options for indoor exercises that are not detrimental to your ability to sleep later in the evening. For example, low-intensity yoga is a great way to relax the body. Sun salutations are a good, rhythmic yoga routine that works the whole body while keeping the heart rate low, and there are multiple types as well as variations if there is a step you are unable to do.

Furthermore, PMR that I mentioned when we talked about relaxation techniques is a good way to exercise the body without causing too much disturbance to sleep. It engages all of your muscles and expends energy while also allowing you to enjoy medical relaxation benefits. Similarly, singing or pretending to yell loudly are also good ways to expend excess energy at bedtime. Even if it does not seem like this is doing much, both activities are actually exercising your lungs, diaphragm, and facial muscles. You can also try simply meditating before bed, or doing in-bed stretches.

My Story

As I continued on my insomnia recovery path, I tried many things to allow me to sleep better. Outside of CBT, I also started to make diet and lifestyle changes that, to my surprise, were incredibly beneficial on how well I felt during the day. I stopped drinking all caffeine and drastically lowered my alcohol intake. I also worked on cutting out processed foods by replacing them with leafy greens. These changes really did improve my sleep quality, and I began to notice certain patterns with my diet and sleep. On days I drank with friends, I felt way more exhausted than on days I did not drink any.

Because of this, I always encourage insomnia sufferers to work on getting the proper nutrients their body needs. Along with consuming healthy foods, I found prayer to be incredibly effective as a way of improving sleep. Praying before going to bed was personally super helpful in relaxing my mind and body, and I highly recommend it to those suffering from insomnia. We'll talk about how to incorporate prayer into your insomnia healing process in the next chapter.

Chapter 10:
Let Go and Let God

"Therefore I tell you, whatever you ask for in prayer, believe that you have received it, and it will be yours." – Mark 11:24

As you know by now, sleep troubles can result from many different points. Emotions are an especially common reason for trouble sleeping, including ones like stress, worry, and anxiety. The presence of these feelings can be incredibly prohibitive when trying to get a good night's sleep. Resentment and grudges can be especially disruptive as well. This is because resentment can raise stress and counteracts some of the principles of relaxation we discussed in an earlier chapter. Factors like this are commonly linked to severely poor sleep quality.

Interestingly enough, those who are religious or spiritual tend to be less depressed, stressed, and anxious than those who are not. Religion and spirituality are very comforting and can provide peace among the most difficult of times, which is why including prayer into a nighttime routine can improve sleep quality. Even if you are not necessarily religious, being able to sacrifice control to a higher being can feel incredibly freeing and reduce or eliminate stress for quite some time.

Prayer and Sleep

Prayer is a meaningful and beneficial way to improve the quality of your sleep. The most notable reason prayer improves sleep is that it lowers stress, anxiety, and resentment along with other negative feelings that can harm our ability to sleep restfully. Prayer also improves physical health as it allows you to relax through forms of meditation and deep breathing, just adding on the benefits of incorporating prayer into your nightly routine. Prayer can also inspire you to be more positive about yourself and what is to come instead of dwelling on negativity before bed. The act of trusting God to care for you during and after prayer is reassuring and the amount of trust you must have for Him inspires healthy mindsets as well. Dedicating a portion of your night to spiritual practices that are meaningful to you are absolutely beneficial to reducing insomnia.

All of these different prayers can seem overwhelming, but fortunately, according to the Bible, there is one key prayer that you can say that is really all-encompassing and beneficial. It is the Lord's Prayer from Mathew 6:9-13. This prayer is as follows:

- "Our Father, who art in heaven, hallowed be thy name; thy kingdom come; thy will be done; on earth as it is in heaven. Give us this day our daily bread. And forgive us our trespasses, as we forgive those who trespass against us. And lead us not into temptation; but deliver us from evil."

If you feel compelled to memorize just one prayer, I highly recommend that that be the one.

Prayers for Comfort and Peace

This section focuses on prayers you can utilize situationally to improve your sleep, depending on what you would like to focus on. Each subsection contains a Bible reading as well as an original prayer I've written. You can combine these, make up your own prayer, or do whatever feels best to encourage prayer as a method for relieving your insomnia.

For When You are Anxious

Bible Reading:

"Therefore I tell you, do not worry about your life, what you will eat or drink; or about your body, what you will wear. Is not life more than food, and the body more than clothes? Look at the birds of the air; they do not sow or reap or store away in barns, and yet your heavenly

Father feeds them. Are you not much more valuable than they? Can any one of you by worrying add a single hour to your life?

And why do you worry about clothes? See how the flowers of the field grow. They do not labor or spin. Yet I tell you that not even Solomon in all his splendor was dressed like one of these. If that is how God clothes the grass of the field, which is here today and tomorrow is thrown into the fire, will he not much more clothe you—you of little faith? So do not worry, saying, 'What shall we eat?' or 'What shall we drink?' or 'What shall we wear?' For the pagans run after all these things, and your heavenly Father knows that you need them. But seek first his kingdom and his righteousness, and all these things will be given to you as well. Therefore do not worry about tomorrow, for tomorrow will worry about itself. Each day has enough trouble of its own."

— Matthew 6:25-34

Prayer: Dear Heavenly Father, thank You for making me in your image. You know me best. You love me best. Please join me right here, and soothe my anxiety. I live to serve You and Your will, and I pray You will cast away my anxiety and give me the strength I need to overcome what is troubling me. In Jesus' Name, Amen.

For When You are Afraid

Bible reading:

"So do not fear, for I am with you; do not be dismayed, for I am your God. I will strengthen you and help you; I will uphold you with my righteous right hand."

— Isaiah 41:10

Prayer: Dear Heavenly Father, on this night I am overcome with fear. It tugs at my heart and overwhelms me, but I look to You for the cure. I pray that You will keep me safe and quell my fears, I pray that You will hold my hand and guide me through whatever comes my way. I believe in You and Your love. Please relieve me of what frightens me, Dear Lord. In Jesus' Name, Amen.

For When You Forgive or Ask for Forgiveness

Forgiveness is especially important to me because holding onto bad feelings for someone is, as mentioned, detrimental to both mental and physical health. I want to take a moment to elaborate on the importance forgiveness has had in my healing journey. Forgiveness is something that I've struggled with before. One of my ex-partners, for example, betrayed me in a way that was unforgivable. For so long I held onto bitterness, contempt, and anger in my heart for him. However, one day I felt compelled to message him and tell them that I forgave him for all his wrongdoings. He never responded, but nonetheless once I did reach out, it felt as if the world had been lifted off my shoulders. I am unable to begin to describe the amount of relief I felt after opening up to forgiveness. If someone in your life has hurt you and you can find the strength to genuinely offer forgiveness, I recommend you do so. Forgiving someone does not mean forgetting, but it does open up so much more for the process of healing once you have done so.

Bible reading:

"Bear with each other and forgive one another if any of you has a grievance against someone. Forgive as the Lord forgave you."

– Colossians 3:13

Prayer: Dear God in Heaven, please grant me the strength and opportunity to forgive and be forgiven. Please take the resentment from my heart so that I may be loving and selfless once again. Please strip me of my desire for revenge, ill-wishes on others, and ill-wishes toward myself. I trust You, God, my one and only Savior, to guide me toward what is right and allow me to overcome the evil tugging at me on this night. I surrender all malicious feelings toward myself and others to You, in hopes that You will allow forgiveness to take its place. In Jesus' Name, Amen.

For When You Need Sleep and Rest

Bible reading:

"In peace I will lie down and sleep, for you alone, Lord, make me dwell in safety."

– Psalm 4:8

Prayer: Dear Lord, as I lay down to rest tonight, I pray that You will ease my mind of all hindrances and allow me to rest. Give me peace to rest so that I may carry on in carrying out Your will and acting in Your Holy Name. In Jesus' Name, Amen.

Additional Prayer: God loves to lavish gifts on His children, and He tells us to ask Him for what we need (Matthew 7:7-11). If you are having trouble falling asleep, ask God to help you get the rest your body needs. Trust Him to care for your needs in His perfect timing. Father, please give me relief from these sleepless nights. I am so tired. In your mercy, please give me the gift of restful sleep. You have filled my heart with joy, more joy than all the riches in the world could bring. I will lie down and sleep in **peace**, for You are with me, and I am safe in Your **love**. I pray in Jesus' name, Amen.

Additional Prayers

As far as prayers I did not write go, I have a lot of recommendations for prayers that you can memorize, write down, or otherwise utilize for peace, sleep, and more. Before I go on with those, though, I have a recommendation for a copy of the Bible that I adore. Personally, I feel that reading the Bible cover to cover is rather ineffective. This version of the Bible instead has an index according to what you need, and then directs you to passages corresponding to what you looked up. It is called The Life Recovery Bible, and I love using it whenever I need guidance from the Bible. If this sounds like it would be beneficial to you, definitely pick yourself up a copy!

The following is a list of just a few prayers I did not write but found that I have held onto as part of my catalog of helpful prayers to revisit:

- "Blessed Jesus, in the comfort of your love, I lay before you the memories that haunt me, the anxieties that perplex me, the despair that frightens me, and my frustration at my inability to think clearly. Help me to discover your forgiveness in my memories and know your peace in my distress. Touch me, O Lord, and fill me with your light and your hope. Amen." (Berry, 2022)
- "Dear God, I know that the first step in all spiritual healing is to believe. I believe! I open my mind and heart believing in your infinite power and possibility. I believe that healing is a dynamic and reachable experience, a reality that can be experienced right now. I maintain a patient and loving attitude, for I believe that your healing activity is now at work in my mind and body. I look forward, with joyful expectation, to the perfect wholeness that you are now bringing into manifestation through me. I believe in your constant expression of perfect good in and through me. I rest in the certainty of your healing power. I know that with you all things are possible. In Jesus Christ's name, Amen."
- "Jesus, I know that when you walked on the Earth, you trod upon hard places, you felt the strain of this world and the pressures of mental torment. So I ask that you would come besides me now, lead me through this time where my mind cannot cope. Help me to find peace and calming inner thoughts. You hold me safe Lord, I trust in you. Amen."
- "Lord, lift me up for Your blessings today. I pray that you will anoint me with strength and self care today, tomorrow, and always. I pray that You will grace me with patience and wisdom. I pray that You will encourage me throughout the day to take the correct steps to walk proudly, and behave well. I pray all of these things in Your name. Amen."
- "May you desire to be healed. May what is wounded in your life be restored to good health. May you be receptive to the ways in which healing needs to happen. May you take good care of yourself. May you extend compassion to all that hurts within your body, mind, and spirit. May you be patient with the time it

takes to heal. May you be aware of the wonders of your body, mind, and spirit and their ability in returning you to good health. May you be open to receive from those who extend kindness, care, and compassion to you. May you rest peacefully under the sheltering wings of divine love, trusting in this gracious presence. May you find little moments of beauty and joy to sustain you. May you keep hope in your heart. Amen."

- "God, have mercy on me. I am sorry I sinned against you and did what is evil in Your sight. In Your unfailing **love** and great compassion, please wash away my sin. I know that you are the only One who can save me from my guilt and make me clean. Create in me a pure heart and a steadfast spirit. Restore to me the joy of your salvation. I ask this in Jesus' name, Amen."

- "I take refuge in You, Lord. I rejoice in Your love, for you see all my troubles and know exactly how I feel. Be merciful to me, Lord, for I am weak and distressed. I feel surrounded and overwhelmed and alone, but I trust in You. You are my God, and You are good. Shelter me in Your presence and be my rock of refuge. In Jesus' name I pray, Amen."

My Story

Spirituality is one of the most important ways I healed my insomnia. This wasn't prescribed to me by any medical professional, but it came to my mind as a solution through trying different methods and reflecting in journals and discussions with my friends. Connecting with God allowed me to let go of all worries, which then let me sleep far better. A lot of people have told me that religion is subjective or unreliable, but I believe with my entire being that God has been and continues to be instrumental in my journey. Without my belief in and dedication to Him, I wholeheartedly believe that I would not be where I am today. God has allowed me to overcome addiction to alcohol, substance abuse, to overcome infertility (gracing me with my beloved daughter), and to rest better at night. Through everything, God has been by my side and I hope that anyone else in need of support can find the strength to turn to God too.

Secular Aid

In my journey with curing my insomnia, God and religion have been the most important thing to my healing process. I truly cannot over exaggerate the impact that Christ has had on my life, and I do encourage anyone who is willing to try and find solace in the Lord the way I have.

However, I also recognize that some people are not religious or do not follow my own religion, and I want this book to be helpful for everyone. I want you to be able to relate and benefit from this book just the same, so I've included a section for secular, spiritual sleep tips that perhaps you can benefit from instead. Again, I cannot express how grateful and appreciative I am for the benefits Christianity has offered me; they have been life changing in just about every sense. If you are willing, I encourage you to try and find a place for God in your heart. Christianity is a very open religion, and I do hope that non-Christians can take my suggestions to heart; God is willing to listen. If that just does not align with you, though, these secular sleep tips are for you!

The first thing I can offer as a recommendation is meditation and prayer, but not in the traditional Christian way. Praying can be used to refer to a lot of things, and if you are not Christian or believe in a different deity, you can still experience benefits from prayer. If you believe, for example, that a higher being exists, or even in the universe as a higher being, pray to them even if you are unable to pinpoint who they are. This allows you to relinquish control and find faith and trust in something higher than yourself, just like I do within my own religion. Meditation is also an excellent way to practice giving up a bit of control and allowing yourself to just be. Both of these options are good for rest and relaxation before bed.

Another thing that I can suggest is herbal remedies if that is something that you are personally willing to try. This can be in the form of baths, teas, essential oil diffusers, etc. Taking a bath with herbs, drinking herbal tea, or diffusing natural oils from an herb can be incredibly beneficial. Just like chamomile tea can help with sleep, so can a lavender and chamomile bath or diffusing the oils from either. This is because the scent or makeup of the herbs are beneficial to relaxing your mind and body. Some people even believe that herbal remedies work because of the energies within the herbs, so if this sounds like something you can get behind, then herbal remedies might be for you. You should not just use any old herb though; there are a few connected with benefits of calm, sleep, and restoration that we are looking for in spiritual aid. Some of those herbs include lavender, chamomile, lemon balm, and rosemary. Others that you can use include valerian and St. John's wort, however you should research these carefully before use– certain herbs like these can interact negatively with medications or cause complications in pregnant people.

A lot of people also state that crystals have been helpful in aiding their sleep. While I personally am unable to testify to the usefulness of crystals in sleep, many report that the energies of the crystal are helpful for relaxing. On a scientific level, it is suggested that crystals work by allowing you to focus your energy and intent on a specific object, so technically you could use anything in place of crystals. Two crystals a lot of people enjoy for sleep include amethyst and rose quartz, both of which are cheap and easy to obtain.

These are just a few of the spiritual alternatives people appreciate for improving their sleep. If these sound enjoyable to you, I recommend doing more research into spiritual sleep tools to see what works best for you.

This chapter has offered various insight into religious practice and the benefits it can provide to those suffering from insomnia. We talked about Christian aspects of sleep benefits, including how prayer and seeking the aid of God can improve your quality of sleep. You also have a few spiritual but secular tools in your kit now just in case you don't follow the same religion as I do. Now, you understand the scientific and spiritual components of prayer that allow it to be so beneficial for healing insomnia, as well as how you can personally implement aspects of spirituality to help with insomnia.

Conclusion

Welcome to the end of the book! Throughout it, you learned about the symptoms, causes, and solutions for insomnia. You now know about what causes your insomnia specifically, how to learn more about your personal insomnia experience, and various strategies to alleviate the symptoms of it. Comfort and knowledge in the science of sleep and insomnia, treatment options, how to be self-aware of your own triggers, CBT and how it or self-guided therapy can benefit you, sleep restriction and stimulus control, cognitive restructuring, sleep hygiene, relaxation, nutrition, and prayer are instrumental in your ability to heal from insomnia.

Combining the main three strategies I've given you–CBT, nutritional values, and prayer–are what cured my insomnia. These methods provided me with restorative sleep that did not rely on medication and healed my insomnia in a holistic manner that improved the health of my mind, body, and soul. Now, every night I go to sleep relaxed, and every morning I wake up well rested and enthusiastic about the day ahead.

It is vital that you realize the process you are making in your journey towards beating insomnia. Success is not immediate, but with patience and consistency I promise that your efforts will pay off. Maintaining a healthy routine of CBT practices, good eating, and prayer are essential in developing and keeping healthy sleep patterns in the long-term, and doing so will increase the overall quality of your life. It is my hope that everyone can use these skills to develop the sleep routine of their dreams, no pun intended. I want each and every one of the people who reads this book to feel inspired and know that they deserve more out of their sleep.

Follow the guidelines and suggestions I've provided and I guarantee that in no time, you will be sleeping well and feeling refreshed every single day. Remember to focus energy on eliminating cognitive distortions, improving your routine and sleep environment, ensuring that your health is in order, and making space in your life for God, and there is no way you can go wrong from there.

If this book has impacted you positively, please consider spreading the love and sharing your thoughts with others online! Your kind words and review will allow others to benefit from this knowledge too. Together we can start a chain of support and help that aids in lowering the harrowing statistics behind people with insomnia. Your support will go so far in spreading healing for everyone who picks up this book.

Thank you for spending this time with me, and I wish you the very sweetest of dreams tonight and every night after!

One-Click Review!

I truly hope you enjoyed "Insomnia Solutions" and that one (or more) of the solutions that worked for me will work for you too! Reviews are SO very important. I would be incredibly thankful if you would please take less than 1 minute to leave a rating/review by clicking:

https://www.amazon.com/review/create-review?&asin=B0BWL8LGY4

If you read a print version, please type the address listed above into your internet browser to be sent directly to the review page for this book (also can go back to the Amazon purchase page, click on "ratings", and then "leave a review"). Thank you in advance for your time and support!

Thank you!

References

American Academy of Sleep Medicine. (2008). *Insomnia.* https://aasm.org/resources/factsheets/insomnia.pdf

American Psychological Association. (2017, July). What Is Cognitive Behavioral Therapy? *American Psychological Association.* https://www.apa.org/ptsd-guideline/patients-and-families/cognitive-behavioral

American Psychological Association. (2023). *Sleep Diary Instructions.* Apa.org. https://www.apa.org/pubs/books/supplemental/pediatric-sleep-problems/Sleep_Diary_Instructions.pdf

Asp, K. (2020, January 22). *Quantity of Sleep Vs Quality of Sleep: Why this is Important?* Www.aastweb.org. https://www.aastweb.org/blog/quantity-of-sleep-vs-quality-of-sleep-why-this-is-important

Bonomo, L. (2020). *Cognitive Behavioral Therapy for Insomnia: How It Works & What to Expect.* Choosing Therapy. https://www.choosingtherapy.com/cbt-for-insomnia/

Bootzin, R. R., & Perlis, M. L. (2011). Stimulus Control Therapy. *Behavioral Treatments for Sleep Disorders,* 21–30. https://doi.org/10.1016/b978-0-12-381522-4.00002-x

Breus, M. (2022, December 13). *Relaxation Techniques for Sleep.* The Sleep Doctor. https://thesleepdoctor.com/sleep-hygiene/relaxation-techniques-for-sleep/

Carney, C. E., Edinger, J. D., Morin, C. M., Manber, R., Rybarczyk, B., Stepanski, E. J., Wright, H., & Lack, L. (2010). Examining maladaptive beliefs about sleep across insomnia patient groups. *Journal of Psychosomatic Research, 68*(1), 57–65. https://doi.org/10.1016/j.jpsychores.2009.08.007

Carroll, A. (2018, April 30). *Parasites and Sleep - Sleep Like a Boss - Sleep Experts for Adults*. Sleep like a Boss - Sleep Experts for Adults. https://sleeplikeaboss.com/parasites-and-sleep/

Centre for Clinical Interventions. (n.d.). *Insomnia and your thinking*. https://www.cci.health.wa.gov.au/~/media/CCI/Mental-Health-Professionals/Sleep/Sleep---Information-Sheets/Sleep-Information-Sheet---03---Insomnia-and-Your-Thinking.pdf

Chambers, D. (2020, October 27). *Avoid These Bad Sleep Habits For A Better Night's Sleep - Sleep Junkie*. Www.sleepjunkie.com. https://www.sleepjunkie.com/bad-sleep-habits/

Cherry, K. (2007, June 16). *The 4 Stages of Sleep (NREM and REM Sleep Cycles)*. Verywell Health; Verywellhealth. https://www.verywellhealth.com/the-four-stages-of-sleep-2795920

Cherry, K. (2022, August 10). *Cognitive behavioral therapy*. Verywell Mind. https://www.verywellmind.com/what-is-cognitive-behavior-therapy-2795747

Cleveland Clinic. (2021, December 3). *Sleep: How Much You Need and Its 4 Stages*. Cleveland Clinic. https://health.clevelandclinic.org/your-complete-guide-to-sleep/

Drevitch, G. (2016). *Therapy Without a Therapist?* Psychology Today. https://www.psychologytoday.com/us/blog/think-act-be/201609/therapy-without-therapist

Elmer, J. (2020, January 8). *Classical Conditioning: How It Works and How It Can Be Applied*. Healthline. https://www.healthline.com/health/classical-conditioning#definition

ENERGY BOOST COLUMN. (2020, September 29). *PART 4: EATING TOO CLOSE TO BEDTIME - TMJ & SLEEP THERAPY CENTRE OF CLEVELAND*. https://clevelandtmjsleep.com/part-4-eating-too-close-to-bedtime/

External Factors that Influence Sleep | Healthy Sleep. (2007, December 18). Healthysleep.med.harvard.edu.

https://healthysleep.med.harvard.edu/healthy/science/how/external-factors

Felix, V. (2020). *Part II: Sleep-Related Thoughts That Are Keeping You Awake.* Cognitive Therapy for Women. http://www.ctwomen.org/blog/2020/3/2/part-ii-sleep-related-thoughts-that-are-keeping-you-awake

Gangwisch et al. (2019). *High glycemic index and glycemic load diets as risk factors for insomnia: analyses from the Women's Health Initiative.* Academic.oup.com. https://academic.oup.com/ajcn/article/111/2/429/5673520?login=false

Gotter, A. (2018, April 20). *4-7-8 Breathing: How It Works, How to Do It, and More.* Healthline. https://www.healthline.com/health/4-7-8-breathing#How-does-the-4-7-8-breathing-technique-work?

Gupta, R. (2016). Presleep thoughts and dysfunctional beliefs in subjects of insomnia with or without depression: Implications for cognitive behavior therapy for insomnia in Indian context. *Indian Journal of Psychiatry, 58*(1), 77. https://doi.org/10.4103/0019-5545.174385

Hull, M. (2021, April 14). *Insomnia Facts & Statistics.* The Recovery Village Drug and Alcohol Rehab. https://www.therecoveryvillage.com/mental-health/insomnia/insomnia-statistics/

Jewell, T., & Hoshaw, C. (2021, November 5). *Diaphragmatic Breathing: Exercises, Techniques, and More.* Healthline. https://www.healthline.com/health/diaphragmatic-breathing#steps

Kaiser Permanente. (n.d.). *What is Sleep Restriction Therapy?* https://thrive.kaiserpermanente.org/care-near-you/northern-california/sanjose/wp-content/uploads/sites/7/2015/10/sleep-restriction-rev2_tcm28-557887.pdf

Lam. (2016, October 22). *Insomnia and Adrenal Fatigue: Why Can't I Sleep When It's Time to go to Bed?* Dr. Lam Coaching - World Renowned Authority on Adrenal Fatigue Recovery.

https://www.drlamcoaching.com/blog/insomnia-and-adrenal-fatigue/

Lamoreux, K., & Raypole, C. (2022). *Insomnia: Causes, Symptoms, Types, and More.* Healthline. https://www.healthline.com/health/insomnia#symptoms

Leech, J. (2022, January 6). *10 Top Benefits of Getting More Sleep.* Healthline. https://www.healthline.com/nutrition/10-reasons-why-good-sleep-is-important#4.-May-strengthen-your-heart

Lefkowitz, C. (2020). *The 3 Ps of Insomnia: How 1 Bad Night Turns Into 100.* Insomnia.Sleep-Disorders.net. https://insomnia.sleep-disorders.net/clinical/three-factors-model

Lewis, M. (2022, August 3). *Heavy metals and insomnia.* Complete Sleep Solu. https://www.thecompletesleepsolution.com/post/heavy-metals-and-insomnia

Meistad, A. (2022). *How the Homeostatic Sleep Drive Works.* Dawn Health. https://www.dawn.health/blog/how-the-homeostatic-sleep-drive-works

National Heart, Lung, and Blood Institute. (2022, March 24). *Sleep Deprivation and Deficiency - What Are Sleep Deprivation and Deficiency? | NHLBI, NIH.* Www.nhlbi.nih.gov. https://www.nhlbi.nih.gov/health/sleep-deprivation

Newsom, R. (2020, October 22). *Cognitive Behavioral Therapy for Insomnia (CBT-I).* Sleep Foundation. https://www.sleepfoundation.org/insomnia/treatment/cognitive-behavioral-therapy-insomnia

Nunez, K. (2019, March 26). *Delayed Sleep Phase Syndrome: Causes, Symptoms & Treatments.* Healthline. https://www.healthline.com/health/sleep-deprivation/delayed-sleep-phase-syndrome

Nunez, K. (2020a, August 10). *Progressive Muscle Relaxation: Benefits, How-To, Technique.* Healthline. https://www.healthline.com/health/progressive-muscle-relaxation#about-pmr

Nunez, K. (2020b, September 10). *Guided Imagery: How To and Benefits for Sleep, Anxiety, More*. Healthline. https://www.healthline.com/health/guided-imagery#benefits

Ong, J. C., Ulmer, C. S., & Manber, R. (2012). Improving sleep with mindfulness and acceptance: A metacognitive model of insomnia. *Behaviour Research and Therapy, 50*(11), 651–660. https://doi.org/10.1016/j.brat.2012.08.001

Pacheco, D. (2022, April 1). *Diabetes and Sleep: Sleep Disturbances & Coping*. Sleep Foundation. https://www.sleepfoundation.org/physical-health/lack-of-sleep-and-diabetes

Procedures. (n.d.). Stanfordhealthcare.org. https://stanfordhealthcare.org/medical-treatments/c/cognitive-behavioral-therapy-insomnia/procedures.html

Radhakrishnan, R. (2022). *What Are the Five Types of Insomnia?* MedicineNet. https://www.medicinenet.com/what_are_the_five_types_of_insomnia/article.htm

Robards, K. (2022, May 31). *What is sleep restriction therapy for insomnia?* Sleep Education. https://sleepeducation.org/sleep-restriction-therapy-insomnia/

Rosenberg, D. C. (2020, December 11). *What is Sleep Restriction Therapy? Does it Work? | Treatment for Insomnia*. Https://Www.sleephealthsolutionsohio.com/. https://www.sleephealthsolutionsohio.com/blog/how-sleep-restriction-therapy-works/

Rossman, J. (2019). Cognitive-Behavioral Therapy for Insomnia: An Effective and Underutilized Treatment for Insomnia. *American Journal of Lifestyle Medicine, 13*(6), 544–547. https://doi.org/10.1177/1559827619867677

Sabatini, S., Ukoumunne, O. C., Ballard, C., Collins, R., Corbett, A., Brooker, H., & Clare, L. (2021). Cross-Sectional and Longitudinal Associations between Subjective Sleep Difficulties and Self-Perceptions of Aging. *Behavioral Sleep*

Medicine, 1–30. https://doi.org/10.1080/15402002.2021.1994405

Self-guided Therapy. (n.d.). Onebright. Retrieved February 4, 2023, from https://onebright.com/our-approach/how-we-deliver/self-guided-therapy/

Session 3 Cognitive Restructuring and Sleep Medication Reduction Techniques. (n.d.). https://www.umassmed.edu/globalassets/psychiatry/cbti/overcoming_insomnia_session_3.pdf

Stanborough, R. (2019, December 18). *Cognitive Distortions: 10 Examples of Distorted Thinking.* Healthline. https://www.healthline.com/health/cognitive-distortions#thought-origins

Stanborough, R. J. (2020, February 4). *Cognitive restructuring: Techniques and examples.* Healthline. https://www.healthline.com/health/cognitive-restructuring#how-does-it-work

Stimulus control. (n.d.). Stanfordhealthcare.org. https://stanfordhealthcare.org/medical-treatments/c/cognitive-behavioral-therapy-insomnia/procedures/stimulus-control.html

Suni, E. (2020a, August 14). *What is Sleep Hygiene?* Sleep Foundation. https://www.sleepfoundation.org/sleep-hygiene

Suni, E. (2020b, September 11). *Mold in the Bedroom: How it Impacts Sleep.* Sleep Foundation. https://www.sleepfoundation.org/bedroom-environment/mold-in-the-bedroom

Suni, E. (2021a, February 8). *Sleep Statistics.* Sleep Foundation. https://www.sleepfoundation.org/how-sleep-works/sleep-facts-statistics

Suni, E. (2021b, March 10). *How Much Sleep Do We Really Need? | National Sleep Foundation* (A. Singh, Ed.). Sleep Foundation. https://www.sleepfoundation.org/how-sleep-works/how-much-sleep-do-we-really-need

Suni, E. (2021c, June 24). *Sleep Deprivation: Causes, Symptoms, & Treatment*. Sleep Foundation. https://www.sleepfoundation.org/sleep-deprivation

Suni, E. (2021d, December 2). *Stages of Sleep: What Happens in a Sleep Cycle*. Sleep Foundation. https://www.sleepfoundation.org/stages-of-sleep

Suni, E. (2023). *What is Circadian Rhythm?* (A. Dimitriu, Ed.). Sleep Foundation. https://www.sleepfoundation.org/circadian-rhythm

Terry, C. (n.d.). *Cooper Aerobics*. Www.cooperaerobics.com. Retrieved February 2, 2023, from https://www.cooperaerobics.com/Health-Tips/Prevention-Plus/Sneaky-Sleep-Disruptors.aspx

The Drive to Sleep and Our Internal Clock | Healthy Sleep. (2007). Healthysleep.med.harvard.edu. https://healthysleep.med.harvard.edu/healthy/science/how/internal-clock

Tinsley, G. (2018). *How Tryptophan Boosts Your Sleep Quality and Mood*. Healthline. https://www.healthline.com/nutrition/tryptophan

Troy, D. (2021). *Sleep Diary*. Sleep Education. https://sleepeducation.org/resources/sleep-diary/

WebMD Editorial Contributors. (2007). *Drugs to Treat Insomnia*. WebMD; WebMD. https://www.webmd.com/sleep-disorders/insomnia-medications

Made in the USA
Middletown, DE
22 September 2023